THE MUTUAL LOVE
OF CHRIST AND HIS PEOPLE

The Mutual Love of Christ and His People

An explanation
of the *Song of Solomon*
for personal devotions and
Bible study groups

PETER MASTERS

THE WAKEMAN TRUST, LONDON

THE MUTUAL LOVE OF CHRIST AND HIS PEOPLE

© Peter Masters 2004

THE WAKEMAN TRUST
(UK Registered Charity)

Website: www.wakemantrust.org

UK Registered Office
38 Walcot Square
London SE11 4TZ

US Office
300 Artino Drive
Oberlin, OH 44074-1263

ISBN 1 870855 40 X

Cover design by Andrew Owen

Printed by Stephens & George, Merthyr Tydfil, UK

Contents

Both audio and video on-line sermons of Dr Masters, preached at the Metropolitan Tabernacle, are available on the Tabernacle's main website: www.MetropolitanTabernacle.org

Audio messages of Sunday and mid-week ministry may be either downloaded or streamed, and video messages are also available for streaming.

Details of currently available audio cassettes, CDs and video CD ROMs are listed on the following website: www.TabernacleBookshop.org

Each verse of the *Song* is printed above the accompanying
explanation with application.

If used for personal devotions, and the reader takes a modest
four verses each day, the *Song* will be completed in a month.
A chapter each day covers the book in eight days.

Whether a week, a month, or more, may the Lord use this
little book to stir many a heart, so that love for Christ
'may abound yet more and more'.

The Mutual Love of Christ and His People

The Secret of the Song
and Members of the 'Cast'

SOLOMON'S *Song of Songs* is a very beautiful poem of tender love, but why is it in the Bible? There is, after all, nothing in the *Song* directly about God or faith or worship, nor is there any specific moral instruction. And who are the two lovers? The answer, and the 'secret' to understanding this remarkable book, is that the characters did not literally exist, because this remarkable poem is an allegory like *The Pilgrim's Progress*, except that the author is the Holy Spirit. It is through picture language that rich spiritual lessons are given. This is the oldest view of how we should understand the *Song*. The great majority of Bible-believing preachers and commentators throughout history have identified the groom as Christ and the bride as His church, and they have shown how the love metaphors prophesy and describe in an amazing way the work of Christ for believers and their response to Him.

For generations the immense value of the *Song* has been recognised in setting out the 'ingredients' of spiritual love. A very different point of view says that this poem celebrates a real love relationship (some say between Solomon and his first wife) in order to present human love at its best and to suggest lessons for courtship and married life. Still another viewpoint sees three people in a love triangle, the young woman, her rustic shepherd lover, and King Solomon who tries to seize her for his harem. We greatly prefer the traditional view for a number of reasons which readers need to know to get the most from the book.

1 The Title Points to Christ

Firstly, the original Hebrew title is *Song of Songs*, meaning the best of all possible songs, or the supreme and most beautiful song ever composed, an extravagant title for the love of ordinary human beings. Such a title best refers to the love of the Son of God for His people and their responding love to Him.

2 Solomon is Not a Model for Marriage

Secondly, Solomon, the inspired author, would hardly be the ideal channel for lessons on love and marriage in view of his having acquired a thousand wives and concubines who turned away his heart from God. The life of the teacher must surely commend the message. If Solomon wrote about his own first courtship and marriage, how could this be described as the best song and put forward as a model when it quickly became a betrayed relationship? A repentant sinner, however, is an acceptable person to write about the mercy of Christ to His church, and Solomon became such a person after his restoration to God (reflected in *Ecclesiastes*).

3 There is No Wedding

A third reason why we must see the *Song* as an allegory of the love between Christ and His church, rather than a manual on married life, is that there is no wedding in it. It is a fact that the bride and groom are viewed throughout the book as *not yet fully* married, this being one of the compelling dramatic features. Modern writers tend to marry the couple off at an early stage so that they may view them as husband and wife, complete with physical intimacy and marital tiffs, but all this is read into the *Song*. The reality is that the bride and groom had engaged in the first stage of an ancient Jewish betrothal, so that they were wholly committed to each other, but they did not yet live together (a situation reflected in *Deuteronomy 20.7*). Today, we would say they were engaged, but the initial betrothal of those days was more binding than modern engagement. Throughout the *Song* the bride and groom are seen waiting for the day of the wedding ceremony with its great marriage supper, and they are still looking forward to it with great desire at the end. This, as we shall see, is powerfully prophetic, providing a picture of the exceptionally close union between believers and their Lord as they wait for His coming at the end of the age, and the great bridal supper of the Lamb. This was perfectly expressed long ago by the outstanding commentator Matthew Henry:

> 'The spouse wishes for a constant intimacy and freedom with the Lord Jesus. She was already betrothed to him, but the nuptials being not yet solemnised and published (the bride, the Lamb's wife, will not be completely ready till His second coming), she was obliged to be shy and to keep at some distance.'

The *Song* is like a drama with several acts, in which we see visits and also times of separation between bride and groom, because she lives in one place and he in another. Even the wedding procession scene (in chapter 3) ends without ceremony or feast because this is the theme of the book – to view the church of Christ in her wedding procession (now) heading for the great day that lies in the future. In the *Song*, therefore, the bride and groom never lie down in intimacy, and it takes hugely imaginative and presumptuous exposition to see them doing so. This 'in between' state of being betrothed, and waiting for the great day of the wedding is the supreme feature of the *Song,* for this makes it relevant to us today, teaching us how to improve and maintain communion with Christ. No wonder C. H. Spurgeon said, 'As a believer draws near to Heaven, this is the book he takes with him.' If we miss this feature, the *Song* becomes chaotic in its order of events, and has nothing to say to our spiritual lives.

4 Love Terms Cannot be Real

A fourth reason for the superiority of the grand old view is that many expressions of admiration used in the *Song* are simply not credible for human love, such as when the groom tells the bride she resembles pharaoh's horses, or that she has a neck like the squat, rough Tower of David, plus other equally jarring descriptions. If, however, the poem is an allegory of the love between Christ and the church, these strange sentiments come to life, describing the privileges and characteristics of saved people. The love poem is only the 'vehicle' for a message. The descriptions were never meant to be wholly realistic, or to be taken literally. As the old saying goes: an allegory says one thing but means another. We must see the deeper meaning.

5 Great Prophecies are Here

A fifth reason for taking the groom to be Christ, and the bride to be the church, is the amount of prophecy which becomes obvious through this interpretation. It is no coincidence that many passages picture well the incarnation of Christ, His saving work, His resurrection, the establishment of the church age, the calling of the Gentiles, and the future heavenly kingdom. To see these events is certainly not fanciful, as we will show. One modern evangelical Bible dictionary says rather surprisingly that 'there is little in the book that is explicitly religious'. This is only true if one takes the fairly modern view that it is a *literal* love story. However, if we take the older view, that this book is a guide to spiritual love, then we see Christ and His work prophesied throughout its eight chapters.

6 Allegory is Solomon's Speciality

A sixth reason for believing that Christ and His church is the subject of this poem is that the Bible tells us that a parable style was the principal feature of Solomon's writings. He issued 3,000 proverbs and 1,005 songs *(1 Kings 4.32)*, many of the proverbs being in the book of *Proverbs*. A proverb is (in the Hebrew) a rule or a comparison, ranging from a short, pithy comparison to a full-size parallel or allegory. While we are told that Solomon specialised in 'comparisons' (teaching truth by means of a fictional story) and also in songs, we are not told that a major part of his work was a marriage guidance manual. We therefore believe that this poem is a combination of song and 'proverb'.[*]

Applying the Song

The *Song* is not only an allegory, it is a *devotional* allegory, intended to exercise and stir our hearts. To explain it we must identify the features of the love of Christ and His people pictured by the words of the groom and the bride. The point behind the words is often fairly obvious, and in places where it is not so obvious great expounders of the past have frequently proposed excellent applications that seem to hit the mark.

It is true that if we take the view that the *Song* is an allegory, we could easily be over-imaginative in drawing parallels with the mutual love of Christ and His people. This has been a fault with

---

[*]A seventh reason for the allegorical approach to the *Song* is its striking similarity of style to *Psalm 45*, 'A Song of Loves', which is so obviously an allegorical poem. To keep this explanatory introduction short, an explanation of this psalm is placed in an appendix on page 113.

some writers from the past whose applications, although usually spiritual and touching, are sometimes far-fetched. In this book every attempt has been made to keep to applications that are plausible, logical, straightforward, and fully in line with teaching elsewhere in the Bible.

All that follows is in line with the tradition of interpretation so loved by the Reformers, the English Puritans and the great eighteenth and nineteenth-century revival preachers. It is also in line with the practice of the Jews, who publicly read this book every year at the Passover, their greatest feast, commemorating Israel's redemption from Egypt, and typifying the redeeming work of Christ. Why ever would they have read a poem about marriage guidance at such a feast? The *Song* is clearly about the love of their expected Redeemer.

The Mutual Love of Christ and His People

Learning Communion With Christ

1 'The song of songs, which is Solomon's.'

T HIS IS DESCRIBED as the very highest song of all, showing that its theme is the greatest manifestation of love ever, the love of God. Ancient Jewish interpreters unhesitatingly decided that the *Song* was about the Messiah, and this would have been the view of all believing Jews before the coming of Christ. Much of the message of the *Song* would have been a great comfort and encouragement to all who waited for Him. Christian expositors soon formed the same view, but with New Testament light and accuracy.

The style of the poem is sometimes reflective, but mainly conversational, as the bride and groom-to-be express their requests and love to each other. As we walk through the fields and glades of these scenes, we remember we are listening to a song, not a lament, and a song that is intended to lift our hearts in devotion and appreciation.

2 'Let him kiss me with the kisses of his mouth: for thy love is better than wine.'

THE BRIDE-TO-BE speaks first (and most throughout the *Song*). She is called 'my love' by the groom (in the *KJV*), whereas she calls him 'my beloved'. Modern Bible translators name the speaker above each verse or group of verses, but this is guesswork and not always reliable. One version calls the groom 'Solomon' throughout and the bride 'the Shulamite' but this assumes that Solomon is the literal groom which is only the translator's opinion. For clarity, and to save on words we will call the woman the bride, or *the church*, and the man the groom, or *Christ*.

The bride (the church) begins in reflective vein, but immediately speaks directly to the groom, as we might do when we move from desire to prayer. She wants his kiss as an assurance that they are united in heart. The kisses of Christ are the redemption-teachings of the Word given, as it were, by His mouth. Here the church mentions her love and enjoyment of the Word, which to her is better than the very best pleasures of the world. The truths that flow from the Word are vastly superior, bringing the message of a Mediator, of atonement, of pardon, of adoption, of eternal and free salvation, and of communion with God, together with a host of promises and assurances. These are the kisses of Christ, representing blessings without parallel in the world. The application for us is that our devotions should begin with the Word and with a deep appreciation of its great truths, as words spoken personally to us by the Lord.

> *Fading is the worldling's pleasure,*
> *All his boasted pomp and show!*
> *Solid joys and lasting treasure,*
> *None but Zion's children know.*
> John Newton

The groom's love is in the plural in Hebrew, signifying the all-surpassing greatness of Christ's feeling for His people. This is the love that brought Him to Calvary, and that follows each believer through life's journey. The bride's longing for love should be represented in our eagerness to reflect in detail on Christ's person and work, in order to *feel* more of His glorious Being and love for us.

3 'Because of the savour of thy good ointments thy name is as ointment poured forth, therefore do the virgins love thee.'

THE FRAGRANCE of the groom's costly ointments or oils is so remarkable and distinctive that the bride is reminded of them by the very mention of his name. When we really love Christ the mention of His name stirs love and gratitude. Costly ointments were used in those times to refresh (suggesting again the promises of Scripture), to mollify and heal wounds (we think of the work of Christ that takes away sin), to anoint kings (we think of our being received into God's family at conversion), and to give pleasure (and we think of the assurance and joy of salvation). His name should remind us of such blessings. Because the ointment is 'poured forth' we are reminded of the sheer abundance of mercy, pardon and life given to saved sinners.

The 'name' of God usually stands for His attributes, and when we remember Christ's divine power, infinity, eternity, purity, knowledge, wisdom and love (which we should frequently do in our devotions) we are moved to amazement that we should be loved by Him. With all this we identify with the words of John Newton:

> How sweet the name of Jesus sounds
> In a believer's ear!
> It soothes his sorrows, heals his wounds,
> And drives away his fear.

In this third verse we meet 'the virgins', or the bride's maidens-in-waiting (elsewhere called the daughters of Jerusalem), who also love the groom. These virgins are treated as learners in the *Song* and characterised as possessing a certain innocence. Who are they?

The following time-honoured view is favoured by this writer. The church has many close followers who, although not yet mature members, sincerely accept the Gospel and the Lord, such as new believers and very earnest seekers. These are strongly attracted to the church, identifying with her and sharing her interests. These are the people represented by the virgins. We will call them her maidens-in-waiting, or her friends.

4 'Draw me, we will run after thee: the king hath brought me into his chambers: we will be glad and rejoice in thee, we will remember thy love more than wine: the upright love thee.'

THE BRIDE speaks both for herself and for her friends asking the groom to draw them. Firstly, this drawing reflects conversion, which is the Lord's initiative, without which our hearts would never have been moved to seek and trust Him. Secondly, it reflects all times of communion with Him, and here the church is seen praying for desire for real communion. How much we need a deep desire to meet with Christ! 'Draw me!' tells us that we must realise we are at a distance without His help. 'We will run!' tells us that we must be determined to respond eagerly and promptly to every opportunity for prayer. 'Run after' is more: it is our promise to obey all His commands, focus our minds on His Word, and work for Him. 'Run after' also reminds us that the Christian life is a race, and that great effort must be exerted to ensure that we come daily to the place of

> 'Draw me, says the believing soul, and then I will not only follow Thee myself as fast as I can, but will bring all mine along with me, I and my house *(Joshua 24.15)*, I and all the transgressors whom I will teach thy ways *(Psalm 51.13)*. Those that put themselves forth will find that their zeal will provoke many. When Philip was drawn to Christ he drew Nathanael. Those that are lively will be active, and will win those that would not be won by the Word.'
>
> — Matthew Henry

Bible study and prayer. The kingly groom responds to the bride's prayer and brings her to visit him in his palace. In other words, in response to her appeals and her pledges the church is brought into communion and deep appreciation of the Lord and the Word. The result is great gladness and assurance, and the application to us is that every day we must call for admission, valuing the privilege of access, and giving Christ a worthy length of time.

The bride next employs a process of comparison, appreciating her blessings by consciously contrasting them with the worldling's 'wine', or benefits and delights, and we must often do the same, lest we take our blessings for granted, or overvalue worldly things.

Says the bride, 'the upright love thee,' hinting that the groom is loved with sincere and genuine love. Bible-believers must be careful not to use greatly excessive expressions of love and appreciation for Christ merely as a matter of habit or 'culture' (a fault with some people) so that their love becomes mere sentimentality. Real love, above all else, is sincere.

5 'I am black, but comely, O ye daughters of Jerusalem, as the tents of Kedar, as the curtains of Solomon.'

THE SONG has scarcely begun when the bride (the church) gives her testimony to her maidens-in-waiting. She is black, she exclaims, speaking not of her ethnicity but of her excessively sun-burned skin acquired as a manual worker in the fields. She realises she is a woman of low station and many blemishes. However, in the eyes of her groom she is beautiful, and this is her testimony. It is ours also in the church of Jesus Christ. We are fallen, sinful people, but clad in Christ's righteousness we are deemed beautiful to Him – 'comely'. On the one hand, the bride (the church) resembles the black goat-hair tents of Kedar, on the other she resembles the costly tapestries of Solomon's palace, these suggesting to us the interwoven doctrines of the faith, and the new nature of saved people. The church's testimony of *grace* is here being explained to seekers and to new believers. Unworthy and condemned, she has been brought into wealth and beauty.

6 'Look not upon me, because I am black, because the sun hath looked upon me: my mother's children were angry with me; they made me the keeper of the vineyards; but mine own vineyard have I not kept.'

THE BRIDE continues her testimony of grace saying, in effect, 'Don't look at me as if I deserved my groom; on the contrary, I am a low-class person of no account, made to work in the vineyards, neglecting my own.' So the saved person looks back and says, 'The world got hold of me and I toiled to do its bidding, serving the things of the world and failing to keep my character in order.' We should never forget our low pre-conversion estate as slaves in the land of Egypt, for this always stirs our love for our Deliverer.

7 'Tell me, O thou whom my soul loveth, where thou feedest, where thou makest thy flock to rest at noon: for why should I be as one that turneth aside by the flocks of thy companions?'

THE BRIDE now makes a plaintive cry to her groom, who in verse 4 was a king, but now is seen as a shepherd, an appropriate occupation for one who represents the great Shepherd of the sheep Who knows His own sheep by name, and Who feeds, protects, watches and leads them. In this verse it appears that the bride has for the moment lost contact with her groom, and is longing to locate him. Where, she asks, is the place where he rests the flock at the heat of noon – a shady place?

When believers are temporarily pushed off-track by temptation, doubt, grief, persecution, hardship or loss they need to recover their communion with the Lord. Here is a good argument to lay before Him when asking for a renewed sense of access to His presence: 'O thou whom my soul loveth'. We mention our love for Him, and our desire for Him rather than anything in this vain world. This will move the Lord to draw us near.

In addition the bride here offers another reason why she needs to be with the groom, namely that she fears being turned aside in loneliness, or falling from assurance and devotion. Some translate her words, 'Why should I be as one who veils herself by the flocks of your fellow-shepherds?' Or 'Why should I be lost in sorrow, cut off from you?' We too may plead our fear of falling away, without assurance of communion with Christ.

8 'If thou know not, O thou fairest among women, go thy way forth by the footsteps of the flock, and feed thy kids beside the shepherds' tents.'

THE SHEPHERD-KING, the groom, now replies to his bride, telling her she is fair and beautiful in his eyes (as we are by grace). If she has lost her way, he tells her, she should obey these directions to find him: she must look out for the tracks of the flock, and follow them. The application to ourselves is obvious. To relocate the Lord at any time, whether a seeker or a veteran Christian, is not complex. Just look for the old paths. Go to Him by way of Calvary and repentance, asking the Spirit to search your heart, giving fresh conviction of sin, together with sincerity and love. Truly turn away from sin, including attitudes such as ingratitude, self-pity, and resentment of others. Reflect on what Christ has done for you, thank Him, and yield your life to Him afresh. Tell Him you will henceforth love, obey and serve Him, and wholeheartedly join the shepherds' tents of those who love Him and engage in His service, for the non-serving believer can hardly expect an increase in felt love and communion. Also, when you go to Him for renewal of spiritual life and vigour, take others with you, the 'kids' or the little goats. In other words, be a witness and a blessing to others, taking them into your daily ministry of intercession, just as the bride of the poem evidently does for her maidens-in-waiting.

9 'I have compared thee, O my love, to a company of horses in Pharaoh's chariots.'

THE GROOM now speaks as if to balance the bride's view of her unworthiness for him as a weather-burnt labourer (verse 5). As the groom says to her, so Christ says to us, 'O my love,' expressing His special interest in us and His atoning work carried out for us. We are not like distant relatives, but loved ones with whom He keeps a constant and deep friendship.

But why the comparison with a company of élite Egyptian horses drawing pharaoh's chariots? Here the old writers had a field-day listing (and rightly) characteristics of truly saved people. These special horses were set aside for royal service, not just kept in a field. They were bought at a high price (*1 Kings 10* mentioning 150 shekels of silver, an immense sum). They were then made fit for their noble station (a good picture of justification). They were well fed (as believers are with the Truth), and majestic in bearing (suggesting distinctive Christian character). They were trained to be unusually strong and courageous to withstand deafening crowds and the tumult of battle (as believers holding to Christ are strong in the trials of life and in witness), and they were quick to respond to the commands of the rein (as believers are to learn and obey). They were also given grooms to care for them (as the church has her pastors).

As we have already observed, for a young woman to be seen as a company of horses is a strange compliment, but for the church to be so described is rich with obvious devotional suggestion.

10 'Thy cheeks are comely with rows of jewels, thy neck with chains of gold.'

WE BELIEVE this continues the description of pharaoh's horses as an illustration of the virtues of the bride. It is the horses that are richly decorated with jewels and gold chains (which was literally true of pharaoh's horses). To put such finery on horses indicated the wealth, dignity, and stature of the pharaoh who was served by them. His rule and might were projected through them.

So with the church, believers are given the glorious ministry of the Word, Gospel labours, and beauty of character (especially seen in unselfishness, self-denial and sincerity). This is the ornamentation of the believer, all of which glorifies Christ.

11 'We will make thee borders of gold with studs of silver.'

THE HORSES were also draped with ornamental blankets of silk and rich tapestry, bordered with priceless studs, probably trophies of great victories or ceremonial emblems from pharaoh's coronation. The church also has a record of great victories since the Day of Pentecost, especially conquests of reformation, revival, and faithfulness in persecution. Individuals, too, bear the evidence of great victories over sin, and all are being made ready for the final coronation and wedding of their victorious Lord.

12 'While the king sitteth at his table, my spikenard sendeth forth the smell thereof.'

NOW THE BRIDE speaks, but once again she is not in the same place as the groom, here described as the king. He is in his palace at his table, and she is presumably at her house waiting for their next meeting. The picture is of the church waiting for Christ. He went to His palace two thousand years ago, and we await His return. However, by the Spirit He entertains us at His table even now, for we sit with Him and hear Him in the Word, and address Him and look upon Him (with the eye of faith) in our devotions.

The bride's spikenard is a costly aromatic ointment from India, and it represents her love for her groom. He is absent, but her love is like a radiant force or commitment, and so is our love for Christ, seen in the fervour of our prayers, obedience and radiating of His name and glory.

13 'A bundle of myrrh is my well-beloved unto me; he shall lie all night betwixt my breasts.'

WITH THE GROOM far away the bride must have something to remind her of him and so she carries a fragrant posy, taking it to bed clutched closely to her heart. With this she cannot forget him. Believers must never leave Christ out of their thoughts for long. Through the day as opportunity arises we are to think of Him, or of some aspect of our service for Him such as an approach to someone in witness. Also, we are to repeatedly ask God's help whether for secular work or for help against sin. In all such prayers we remember Christ, and ask in His name. The hymnwriter Frances Ridley Havergal determined that her last thoughts at night and her first on waking would be about Christ.

We think of Him to revive our flagging spirits, and we think of Him to sanctify heartache. We think of Him to overpower the alluring aroma of covetous desires. We keep His interests always on our minds, and while doing this we can never be unfaithful, allowing our desires to roam to earthly things. All this we learn from the posy of myrrh, the bride's reminder of her groom.

14 'My beloved is unto me as a cluster of camphire in the vineyards of Engedi.'

CONTINUING the thought, the bride takes a cluster of camphire (henna blooms), possibly a figure for a bunch of the very best grapes. If so, as she plucks and eats she is reminded of having shared such fruit with the groom, and it is like being with him. So it is for the church or the individual believer who reflects on Christ's fruits. He is not present in His person, but we reflect on what He has done for us, and we are moved to love Him. We learn of the salvation and imputed righteousness of Christ, but do we 'take it' by thanking Him every day? Our sin has been cast into the vast ocean of God's forgetfulness, but do we praise Him daily? We experience His powerful deeds in answer to our prayers, but do we 'take them' by praising Him in our subsequent daily prayers? To know anything of the presence of Christ in our lives we must be engaged in daily taking of the fruit of His glorious work for us, and reflecting on it.

15 'Behold, thou art fair, my love; behold, thou art fair; thou hast doves' eyes.'

THE KING, the groom, now speaks of the beauty of the bride, indicating the pleasure that Christ takes in the church of His making. The beauty of Christ's people is seen in their unreserved belief in His Word, their changed lives, their obedience to Him, their love and service for Him, and their spiritual graces (soon to be listed). Most of all, probably, believers are beautiful to Christ because He sees what they will be in glory when He has perfected them. Specifically the bride is applauded for her 'dove's eyes', alert, observant and docile or non-argumentative toward God. Old writers point out that the eye of the dove is not bent on prey, as the eagle's or the hawk's, but is non-vindictive, and sympathetic. Do we reflect this?

16 'Behold, thou art fair, my beloved, yea, pleasant: also our bed is green.'

THE BRIDE responds to the groom, exclaiming that he has beauty not only in appearance but also in manner (his pleasantness), for he exercises grace, kindness and gentleness towards all. Christ has both beauty of character and of deportment, and we should resemble Him. The bride refers to their bed, not meaning the place where they lie together, for they are not yet fully married, but signifying the secure and happy future that lies ahead when they do live together. The 'bed' is green, not in the sense that they will lie down in the field, but in the figurative sense that their union will flourish and advance like a growing plant. The Hebrew word here actually means an arch or canopy, referring possibly to the beautiful boughs under which they walked, making them think of their future marital happiness. As believers we should reflect often on the church's spiritual environment, for we walk with Christ in the most pleasant places and have the most glorious future prospects.

17 'The beams of our house are cedar, and our rafters of fir.'

THE BRIDE continues (although the groom could be the speaker here). Some modern writers (surely mistakenly) take this verse to mean that the lovers, who they think have been lying together in the grass, now say that their house is the cedars and firs around them. Faintly plausible as this may seem it sees the yet unmarried bride and groom living dangerously and over-intimately, anticipating their marital privileges. Clearly their 'house' (the Hebrew is actually plural) is a figure of their hopes and dreams for the future. It simply means that their union will be spacious, glorious, happy and enduring. The tallest of trees will be needed for the beams, so great is the span of this house, and the roof will be supported by joists of fir, the most pleasantly scented and rot-free of the trees available. It will be an amazing house for size and splendour, and we too look forward to the eternal, heavenly house that follows the bridal supper of the Lamb.

However, even now the kingdom of Christ is such a house. On Christ, the foundation, are built strong walls with windows that stream with light. The large rooms will accommodate the great fruit of the Gospel, and will allow rich fellowship between the occupants. Such a large house will store countless family treasures – memories of spiritual victories and experiences that will be carried one day into eternity.

The Mutual Love of Christ and His People

Prophecy of a New Era

1 'I am the rose of Sharon, and the lily of the valleys.'

WHO IS THE speaker of these famous words? Among the old writers the most popular answer is – the groom. Among modern writers it is the bride. (One recent study-Bible dismisses the idea that the groom is speaking with near derision.) However, we believe it is undoubtedly the groom, firstly on account of the words, 'I am'. The ancient name of God is 'I am that I am'. We are reminded also of the seven 'I am's' of the *Gospel of John* – I am the bread of life; the light of the world; the door; the good shepherd; the resurrection and the life; the way, the truth and the life; and the vine. The emphatically spoken 'I am' in this allegorical poem is a singularly resonant term which sits best on the lips of the groom, who pictures Christ. Secondly, it is unlikely that the bride would sing her own praise in such an extravagant way, she never does elsewhere.

Thirdly, there is far greater significance in the rose and lily if they refer to Christ, than if they refer to the church.

The groom, representing Christ, uses the rose and lily to describe His coming humanity and humiliation. This prophetic meaning was no doubt obscure to all but the most spiritual of Jews, but with New Testament light it is rich and clear to us. The rose of Sharon is the very best. It is delicate, picturing Christ coming in human flesh, and although it lives on the driest soil it possesses unparalleled splendour, picturing Christ, the perfect Man, living in a barren, sin-sick world. We have read that the Jews of old used a special prayer for Sharon because it had such inhospitable soil. They prayed that the people's houses would not become their graves.

The lily of the valleys depicts the purity of Christ in His 'valley', which is His time of humiliation on the earth. (In the next verse the church will be seen reflecting this.) The key point is that the bride must appreciate the virtues revealed by the groom, admiring them, contemplating them and enjoying them. How often believers become too preoccupied with life to pause and think about Christ and to reflect on His lovingkindness and mighty work. Do we express appreciation of His glorious person and work *in words* when we pray? Do we think, and wonder and adore? Just as the groom speaks these words in the *Song*, so Christ reveals His nature and redeeming work in the Bible. This inspired Word should be the stimulation for our daily

> 'Christ may be said to be the lily of the valleys because of His wonderful humility and condescension in assuming our nature, suffering in our stead, and in His humbling Himself to the death of the cross for us. His whole life was one continuous sequence of humility. Christ on earth did not appear as the lofty cedar, but as the lowly lily, and though He is the high and lofty One in His divine nature, yet He condescends to dwell with such who are of a humble and contrite spirit.'
>
> – John Gill

response of admiration, gratitude, obligation and love.

2 'As the lily among thorns, so is my love among the daughters.'

THE GROOM, Christ, sees the church holding up the cause of godliness among the thorns of this world; amidst all the evil and hostility toward Himself. The church, even if numerically outnumbered, is both more conspicuous (for virtue) and more highly scented (for God's delight) than the world, but, like the lily, she is vulnerable to being choked. If she stands firm she will never resemble thorns or acquire barbs. She will be conspicuous and influential in countless lives as long as she never relaxes her witness.

3 'As the apple tree among the trees of the wood, so is my beloved among the sons. I sat down under his shadow with great delight, and his fruit was sweet to my taste.'

THE BRIDE here begins to respond, comparing the groom to a tree, not as tall, yet superior to all others in the forest for fruit. So Christ is far, far better than all that this world can offer, but, once again, His benefits must be plucked and eaten by seekers and by long-standing believers alike. To be saved, yet to neglect prayer, Bible study, reflection, and service for Christ (which proves His helping power) is to fail to take the fruit and obtain the blessing.

The people of God delight to sit in Christ's shade, taking refuge in Calvary from the burning conscience, and taking shelter in prayer from persecution, distress, and temptation. They love also the calm shade of assurance and certainty, comforts which grow and deepen when the Lord is frequently 'in view' in devotions. Frances Ridley Havergal was inspired by this verse to pen her well-known words:

Sit down beneath His shadow,
And rest with great delight;
The faith that now beholds Him
Is pledge of future sight.

Bring every weary burden,
Thy sin, thy fear, thy grief;
He calls the heavy laden,
And gives them kind relief.

A little while, though parted,
Remember, wait and love,
Until He comes in glory,
Until we meet above.

4 'He brought me to the banqueting house, and his banner over me was love.'

THE BRIDE reflects on what the groom has already done for her in taking her to a great banquet, perhaps part of their initial betrothal ceremony. The banquet stands for salvation, or for the church where the plan of salvation is spread out and the very best of spiritual experiences are given to rejoicing guests. But how did she get there? Obviously in a carriage, not mentioned but implied, sitting under a streaming royal standard bearing the words – 'The Victory of Love'. Love drew us also, for Christ saw our condition, pitied us, went to Calvary for us, conquered Satan, and called us to follow Him.

I've found a Friend, O, such a Friend!
He loved me ere I knew Him;
He drew me with the cords of love,
And thus He bound me to Him.

James Grindlay Small

5 'Stay me with flagons, comfort me with apples: for I am sick of love.'

'STAY ME,' she calls, because love has made her faint, not with flagons but with pressed flowers (a better translation) for their reviving scent or, as some translate it, raisin cakes, for reviving energy. Flowers seems more likely. The Hebrew word translated 'flagons' indicates something pressed.

We too may become 'faint' with love. Sometimes we feel over-whelmed by mercy and grace, and then we wonder (especially when first converted) how it can be true that Christ should do so much for us. It is all so glorious, free, and unexpected that even assurance can be shaken. It is all too good to be true, and we fear to lose Christ Who loves us.

6 'His left hand is under my head, and his right hand doth embrace me.'

HOWEVER, the bride is held from swooning and falling, and gently laid down to rest, picturing the support of renewed assurance and peace ministered directly by Christ. The important point is that we obtain rest only at His hands. If assurance wavers, or troubles spoil communion with Christ, we may, of course, obtain advice from other believers, but for real comfort we must reflect on salvation, and Calvary, and the promises. Entertainment will never restore our peace. This can only temporarily and imperfectly blot out some of the troubles. Christian company may help, but not enough. Only our own thinking on Christ's person and work, plus prayer for help, will bring us to peace.

The groom's left hand under the head suggests Christ's comfort to the mind, and his right hand safely holding the body suggests Christ's strengthening of the believer.

7 'I charge you, O ye daughters of Jerusalem, by the roes, and by the hinds of the field, that ye stir not up, nor awake my love, till he please.'

THE GROOM (Christ) now speaks to the maidens charging them very solemnly not to wake his bride, who in the previous verse is left in his arms, evidently asleep. The KJV says 'till he please', but the Hebrew should ideally be translated 'till she please' (the Hebrew verb being feminine). In other words, Christ wants the church to have undisturbed peace in His love. Bear in mind that this is a pic-ture of the church in her relationship with Christ, not in her battle for the Gospel in a hostile world. Spiritually, the church should have a strong sense of blessedness always, despite trials from outside.

But why should Christ command the maidens about this? If we are correct in thinking that they represent young believers or seekers then the following scene emerges. New converts and seekers may easily strain the spiritual peace of the church by being tempted into sin, and especially into worldliness. Or they may in their immaturity chase after novelties and become superficial. They may also find obedience to the rule of Scripture irksome after the liberal self-determination of the unsaved life. But Christ charges them not to go astray, and He does so in this way. He settles them down under a sense of obligation to obey and please Him, giving them an instinct for what is right, by which they realise that worldliness is wrong and feel keenly the authority of the Word of God. Seekers or new converts who lack this instinct and do whatever they like probably lack any real work of the Spirit in their hearts, because grace always brings about a willingness to obey God, and an active conscience. It is the Lord Who makes converts a source of joy to the church, rather than a source of unrest and anxiety.

Why should the groom charge the maidens to keep the peace of the bride 'by the roes, and by the hinds'? Most probably these energetic animals that leap and bound so easily across the dangerous rocky terrain of the mountains picture victorious spiritual advance and liberty. It is as if Christ is saying to the young in faith, 'In the interests of your unhindered spiritual growth, joy and victory, do not disturb the peace of God's family with sinful and worldly ideas.'

One aspect of the church's life is peace, and another is militant wakefulness because she is also the bearer of the Gospel and the Lord's mouthpiece in the world. The two aspects – peace and militancy – are pictured by sleeping and waking in this verse. As churches and as individual believers we must exhibit both to please Christ our Lord.

8 'The voice of my beloved! behold, he cometh leaping upon the mountains, skipping upon the hills.'

NOW THE BRIDE, the church, speaks, making two points. First, she exclaims that she hears the voice of the groom, and second, that she sees him coming. The voice of Christ is always recognised by true believers and sincere churches, in that they *feel* the authority of the Word and are ready to obey. If it corrects and convicts they meekly accept it, and if it spells out a duty they gladly comply. It is a bad sign when professing Christians will not listen to the Word and go to great lengths to justify their evasion. Surely they must either be false converts, or badly backslidden. True believers value the Word and look to it always for a spiritual and moral message. They have felt its power in their lives in conversion, and love its depths and perfections.

'Christ comes surmounting all the difficulties that lay in His way, making nothing of the discouragements He was to break through: the curse of the law and the death of the cross. All the powers of darkness must be grappled with but by the determination of His love these great mountains became plains.'

– Matthew Henry

In the second part of verse 8 the groom is seen leaping and bounding over the mountainous terrain as a roe or young hart, the language of effortless victory. No matter how hard the circumstances of believers or churches, Christ can approach (spiritually) with ease as the all-powerful, risen Lord, and He will come swiftly to strengthen, help, assure, and also to challenge. Like the bride, the believer both hears Christ's voice, and sees Him with the eye of faith. Whatever our situation we must 'see' Him by believing that He is near. It is by our faith that He manifests Himself unto us.

However, there is something of even greater significance here because we are given in these verses a prophecy of the two comings of Christ, firstly to bring salvation and secondly to appear at the end of the age. The church hears the voice of the Lord speaking about His coming through the prophets. Then she sees Him in the incarnation.

9 'My beloved is like a roe or a young hart: behold, he standeth behind our wall, he looketh forth at the windows, shewing himself through the lattice.'

WE SHALL take, first, the coming of the groom as a prophecy of how Christ would come to earth to atone for His people and establish the Gospel age. He stands behind or outside the wall of the house or compound, and if the bride cannot see him herself, she has word (from a servant perhaps) that he is there. This is reflected in the ministry of John the Baptist, the voice crying in the wilderness to announce the Lord's coming. Then the groom looks through the window at his bride, perhaps depicting Christ contemplating the great host of people for whom He would die. Then the groom shows himself fully, this representing Christ coming to embark on His public ministry, demonstrating His divine power in miracles and authoritative teaching, and also in His death, resurrection and ascension. Immanuel – God with us – is the scene before us in this verse. Matthew Henry delightfully adds:

'They saw Him looking through the windows of the ceremonial institutions, and smiling through those lattices . . . Christ revealed Himself to them and gave them intimations and earnests of His grace.'

10 'My beloved spake, and said unto me, Rise up, my love, my fair one, and come away.'

THE GROOM then calls the bride away – just as Christ called His truly converted people out of the Jewish church into the new era. He called them out of the mixed multitude, out of the deadness of the ceremonial law, and out of the exclusivity of Judaism.

However, there is a further application of the call of the groom, both to an individual believer and to a church. This call is heard by the individual at conversion: 'Arise from spiritual death, come away from your old life and from the world, and let us go together into a new life.' It is a call to separate and to follow a sanctified and spiritual lifestyle. The believer may hear this call often on life's journey, whenever he succumbs to sleepiness, complacency, or preoccupation with present, material matters. 'Rise up from all that,' says the Lord, 'and come away to purposeful service and the winning of lost souls. Come away to mission, to closer communion, to greater learning and discovery of spiritual things, and to holiness.'

The bride is called 'my love, my fair one', reminding us that this is a most gracious call of love and affection to those made fair by the inestimable privilege of the imputed righteousness of Christ.

11 'For, lo, the winter is past, the rain is over and gone.'

HERE IS the pleading reasoning that urges the bride to heed the groom's call to come away, and it is all about the coming of spring. The spring came, first of all, with the resurrection and ascension of the Lord and the Day of Pentecost, when a new and glorious order began for God's people. The long years of lifelessness – the winter time of the Old Testament church – were over, and grace flooded the new church in abundance. In the light of this new dawn, the call to the church was, 'Arise, leave the old order, come out of the physical Temple.' The New Testament call anticipated in this love poem is also found in the prophets:

> 'Arise, shine; for thy light is come, and the glory of the Lord is risen upon thee . . . and the Gentiles shall come to thy light, and kings to the brightness of thy rising' *(Isaiah 60.1-3).*

It is so much easier to travel in the spring, when the heavy rains are over, the rivers are no longer swollen, and the ground is firmer.

So the Gospel flew to the nations once the new age arrived. Isaac Watts wrote:

The Jewish wintry state is gone,
The mists are fled, the spring comes on.

This call of the Lord to come away at spring time applies also to present day believers and churches in several ways. Perhaps we have been through a period of hardship, illness, grief, persecution or even backsliding and correction. But now the dark winter has come to an end, and the call of Christ comes to us once more to take advantage of new and better conditions and recommit ourselves wholly to Him and His service.

It may be that a local church has been through a hard winter in some way. Sowing and reaping has drawn to a halt, or perhaps in a pioneer period there have been very few labourers and few recruits. But now things are a little better, and a new surge of effort is called for. Improved circumstances are further described in the next verse.

12 'The flowers appear on the earth; the time of the singing of birds is come, and the voice of the turtle is heard in our land.'

FLOWERS of fellowship begin to bloom out of a deeper under-standing of Truth. New seekers come into bud, showing promise of eternal fruit. Perhaps saved youngsters, at first resented in their unbelieving families, begin to find acceptance and interest developing. It is a time for the singing of birds, for deeper gratitude and praise, for the building of nests, or the framing of schemes of witness and outreach. Also, the voice of the dove is heard, meaning, perhaps, that the Gospel of peace is being preached, and Christians must take full advantage of it. Perhaps a persuasive evangelist has come to the pulpit, or a soul-hungry Sunday School leader has emerged, and God's people must recognise the season of opportunity, and respond to the task of bringing in others to hear.

13 'The fig tree putteth forth her green figs, and the vines with the tender grape give a good smell. Arise, my love, my fair one, and come away.'

AT THE END of this appeal to come away at spring time, the groom utters the words taken up by Christ (the antitype):

'Now learn a parable of the fig tree; When his branch is yet tender, and putteth forth leaves, ye know that summer is nigh: so likewise ye, when ye shall see all these things, know that it is near, even at the doors. Verily I say unto you, This generation shall not pass, till all these things be fulfilled' *(Matthew 24.32-34)*.

These words are part of the momentous passage in which the Lord speaks both of the beginning and the ending of the church age. The 'parable' of the fig tree applies to the beginning, namely His work to liberate souls on Calvary and so inaugurate the new age.

The groom's words in verse 13 of the *Song* are firstly, therefore, predictive of Christ's coming. Secondly, for today, the green figs and the fragrance of the tender grape suggest Christ's encouraging, fruit-bearing promises, such as – 'Herein is my Father glorified, that ye bear much fruit,' and 'I have chosen you . . . that ye should go and bring forth fruit.' He promises that He will be with us in our witness and that the Spirit will work in hearts and souls will be saved. In the light of these blessings we are once more told to arise, and come away from slumber and walk in commitment and service. He calls the church, 'My love', indicating His desire and delight to use her. 'Come away!' He calls, from self and from the world, to the fullest engagement with Himself.

14 'O my dove, that art in the clefts of the rock, in the secret places of the stairs, let me see thy countenance, let me hear thy voice; for sweet is thy voice, and thy countenance is comely.'

NOW THE GROOM calls the bride his dove, the characteristics of doves being listed by many of the old writers, and shown to picture believers. They love cleanliness, we are told, carefully cleaning all dung out of their nests, and here the application is obvious. By choice they eat grain (rather than worms or rubbish), are innocent and harmless, are very social birds, and, of course, they fly, indicating the believer's ability to fly above trials by prayer. Doves, however, are vulnerable in the hierarchy of birds, being oppressed by birds of prey. They may be fearful, calling out with an appealing voice, yet these are the believers whom Christ so loves. He delights to look upon our born-again characteristics, and to see us acknowledging our needs and depending upon Him.

In this verse the dove hides in the clefts of the rocks, the crags of the mountains, and who of us cannot see the imagery of Calvary first employed in *Exodus 33.22*, where Moses was placed in the cleft of a rock while the Lord, in His glory, passed by. Used again in *Isaiah 32.2*, Christ is seen as a hiding place from the wind, and as 'the shadow of a great rock in a weary land'.

Christ is that great rock once riven for us when the wrath of God against sin was poured out upon Him. In Him we have an infallible atonement, an unshakeable forgiveness, an indestructible imputed righteousness, an impregnable defence, and an everlasting life.

In the second part of the verse the groom desires to see the face of the bride, and to hear her voice. So Christ, in astonishing condescension and kindness, loves to see our faces upturned to Him in adoration and prayer, and to hear our petitions. 'Look up to Me!' He says. And we must respond to Him, for He has purchased us from slavery and death, and made us precious in His sight. We must in all things lean on Him, speak His praise, thank Him and desire Him, expressing all these attitudes with a 'sweet' voice (which in Hebrew means an agreeable or pleasurable voice). The believer's voice is harsh and discordant to Christ when it is proud, self-reliant, or resentful, but the sweet voice is one that is repentant, thankful, adoring, dependent and dedicated. Christ loves the distinctive tone of faith and the melody of intercessory prayer. Our literal voices

may rasp and croak, but our spiritual voices, rightly used, are music
to the Lord.

15 'Take us the foxes, the little foxes, that spoil the vines: for our vines
have tender grapes.'

THERE IS here something that the groom must ask of the bride;
something she must do for him. She is to catch the little foxes
that ruin the vines. This pictures the command Christ gives to
believers and churches to bring out of their holes the sins that
impede the fruits of holiness and of soul-winning. Sin, like the fox,
is crafty, twisting in all directions, and if left unmortified it will strip
the character of everything good.

These foxes include false teaching and all worldly influences which
will ruin our own spiritual progress and also that of others. Christ
is here depicted as saying to the church, 'Protect the vines and the
tender grapes; bring vulnerable teenagers and children from this
atheistic world where they live among the moral wolves of present-
day culture, and draw these children into Sunday Schools and youth
classes.'

But we are not to forget the foxes that gnaw and tear at our personal vine. We must all arrest wrong appetites, passions, tempers,
unkind, selfish or lazy schemes, together with fits of pride, and all
other thoughts and deeds that lay waste the Lord's work in us.

The bride, very much in love, will do anything she can to please
the groom, and we too will arrest the stirrings of sin because we love
Christ and are amazed and overwhelmed at His love for us. The
most successful strides in sanctification (by the help of the Spirit)
are made when we are motivated and energised by love for Him.

C. H. Spurgeon identified the tender grapes of Christ, the true
vine, as being the work of conversion. He listed the fruits as:
(1) secret mourning for sin; (2) humble faith in Christ; (3) a genuine change of life; (4) secret devotion; and (5) simple love. The

grapes smell, he said, of sincerity, teachability, and joy. Spurgeon identified the foxes that would spoil these fruits as people who discourage new converts by any means, or who cause them to doubt, or who draw them back into the world. The vines must be protected, and the foxes denied further spoil.

16 'My beloved is mine, and I am his: he feedeth among the lilies.'

THE BRIDE says these beautiful words to herself, and it is apparent that 'engagement' promises have been made, the first stage of betrothal in those times. The couple did not yet share their lives, but would be bound by these promises, and now had a right to each other. The groom had evidently given himself to her, picturing Christ giving and pledging Himself to His people at His first coming, leading to the 'engagement' period preceding the great marriage supper of the Lamb (at His second coming).

The groom's heart is full of love for his bride, as Christ's is for the church. The bride being poor, the groom has provided everything for their union, just as Christ has for ours by His atoning work on Calvary, and the giving of His righteousness. The groom is his bride's for ever, as Christ is our Lord eternally. Not only the groom, but all he has, is now the bride's, and, similarly, with Christ we become the beneficiaries and sharers of all His wisdom, power, work (of redemption), guardian care, and future reign.

In return, the bride gives herself to the groom. Because Christ is ours, we are His. Lost in His love we say, 'I give myself to Thee.' We yield ourselves to be wholly at His disposal. We are His by purchase at Calvary; by conquest as He worked irresistibly in our heart; and by surrender, when we cried out for mercy and life, and submitted to His rule. We are no longer our own.

How sad it is that nowadays so many Christians do not want to be wholly for the Lord, thinking this to be 'legalism'. They want to have whatever they desire, and do whatever they like. My career is for me, they say, and my leisure for my pleasure. But real love takes the view that our time, energies, loyalty, abilities, and resources are not our own but *His,* for we belong to Him. His interests are our interests, and we will not give away our hearts to other things.

In this verse the groom is absent, feeding his flock among the lilies, but the bride knows she is in his heart. She thinks of him constantly, cherishing the memory of his every word. He is Christ, and she is the church on earth, living at present by the Word, and looking forward to the great day of the wedding. Numerous hymnwriters have been moved to turn the key words into verse, of which we quote two:

> *I lift my heart to Thee,*
> *Saviour divine;*
> *For Thou art all to me,*
> *And I am Thine.*
> *Is there on earth a closer bond than this:*
> *That my Belovèd's mine, and I am His?*
> Charles E. Mudie

> *While here, alas! I know but half His love,*
> *But half discern Him, and but half adore;*
> *But when I meet Him in the realms above,*
> *I hope to love Him better, praise Him more,*
> *And feel, and tell, amid the choir divine,*
> *How fully I am His, and He is mine.*
> Henry Francis Lyte

17 'Until the day break, and the shadows flee away, turn, my beloved, and be thou like a roe or a young hart upon the mountains of Bether.'

THE BRIDE, the church, is determined to maintain her love for her groom until the day they will be gloriously united. That is the day to which she looks, and she will show unwavering faithfulness, fuelled by love, until the moment comes. For us, this is the dawn of eternal day when our Lord shall return. The bride is certain her day will come and the groom will be waiting for her, and surely the doctrine of final perseverance is to be seen here. Then will come the greatest adventure imaginable for the human soul: the revelation of all things, the commencement of eternal glory, and the day of meeting with the Lord (and also with all the saints who have gone before).

The shadows of sin and disobedience will flee – the last vestiges of our rebellion. The scourges of aging, sickness and death will cease, together with all the heartache, war, fear, and oppression of this evil world. Unbelief, scorn, ingratitude, and all that obscures the Lord from our view in this life will be no more.

'Come back soon for me,' calls the bride, or the church. 'Turn, and return for me. Come like the agile hart across the mountains of ravines and division' (the meaning of Bether). 'Speed the day of Thy return, because we so desire the Lord we love, and we pine for Thee, and long to see Thee, on that great and wonderful day.'

The Mutual Love of Christ and His People

CHAPTER

3

Assurance Lost and Regained

1 'By night on my bed I sought him whom my soul loveth: I sought him, but I found him not.'

IS THIS a dream? Does the bride have nightmares? (The Hebrew is literally 'by nights' or 'night after night'.) Does she dream that she has lost her groom? Or was she expecting a visit, and being sure he had arrived in town was unable to sleep until she saw him? For the church, this present age is the time of night when the full presence of Christ is not available to us and we must walk by faith. For this reason assurance sometimes runs low, spiritual experience cools, and zeal is eroded. Reference to the bride's bed may suggest a cause, namely that we are on a 'bed' of excessive ease and comfort, or of spiritual laziness. Whatever the reason, we say with *Psalm 30.7*, 'Thou didst hide thy face, and I was troubled.' Anxiously, we try to get back to real and heartfelt communion with the Lord, but our efforts sometimes seem to fail.

2 'I will rise now, and go about the city in the streets, and in the broad ways I will seek him whom my soul loveth: I sought him, but I found him not.'

IT MAY BE we do not even attempt to get back to where we were, continuing voluntarily in a low spiritual state, but the bride in this love poem goes anxiously through the city searching, a picture of believers seeking renewed spiritual well-being through advice and companionship with other Christians. When spiritually low, some go further, venturing into the 'broad ways' of trying other churches, or books and cassettes from afar, or even resorting to contemporary Christian music. Some try earthly remedies like a change of job or a new place to live or a special earthly friend. But the broad ways of the city will not reveal the Saviour.

3 'The watchmen that go about the city found me: to whom I said, Saw ye him whom my soul loveth?'

THE WATCHMEN illustrate pastors and other spiritual shepherds who watch for souls. (They are Isaiah's watchmen on the wall.) Chiefly through applied preaching of the Word, watchmen 'find' and help troubled souls, and while there is no mention of their having helped the bride in this case, they clearly did, because very soon afterwards she found her groom. A pastor cannot himself re-establish a believer in a close walk with Christ, but he can point out the direction. Some believers seek too much from preachers, imagining that deeply emotional preaching might lift their soul. But the truth and counsel of the Word must be understood and

'By *city* is meant here the church of God, which is frequently called so in Scripture. By *watchmen* is meant the true ministers of the Gospel, called prophets under the Old Testament; apostles and faithful teachers under the New. Watchmen found me and fell upon the subject of my care and condition in their sermons, and exactly spoke to my case.'

– John Gill

applied by the believer to his own case before there can be a benefit.

4 'It was but a little that I passed from them, but I found him whom my soul loveth: I held him, and would not let him go, until I had brought him into my mother's house, and into the chamber of her that conceived me.'

HAVING GONE only a few yards from the watchmen, the bride finds her love. So, we take the Word to heart and seek Christ afresh by faith, by recommitment, by yieldedness, by obedience, by thankfulness and love, and by renewed effort in His service. None of these should be omitted. Then we find Him again. The bride now holds her groom tightly, in deep earnestness, and so appreciates him that she will not let him go, and we too, having renewed our communion with Christ value Him as never before.

The bride takes the groom home, not to sleep, but to spend time in conversation, using the only private chamber in her rustic home, her mother's room. As far as we are concerned, having re-established close communion with Christ, we take Him back to church with us (our family home) and share our joy and our reanimated zeal in the service of our fellowship. Joy renewed is not for private pleasure only, nor for mere emotional self-indulgence. It is to be our contribution to the life of our spiritual family.

5 'I charge you, O ye daughters of Jerusalem, by the roes, and by the hinds of the field, that ye stir not up, nor awake my love, till he please.'

THE WORDS of chapter 2 verse 7 are repeated here, for the bride (the church) now has peace once again, and it must not be disturbed for the time being. Christ, by His great kindness, usually restores the joy of our salvation in a stable way, preserving us from any immediate fresh disturbance so that we have a little time to grow stronger in devotion and service before the next great test or trial.

6 'Who is this that cometh out of the wilderness like pillars of smoke, perfumed with myrrh and frankincense, with all powders of the merchant?'

THE SCENE now changes dramatically to that of a wedding procession, in which a great king and his bride approach the city for marriage. The speakers are either the maidens-in-waiting, or other unnamed bystanders. Modern translations tend to link this verse with the next, as though Solomon was in view. But in the phrase, 'Who is this?' the word 'this' is feminine, showing that the bride is seen first. The wilderness refers here to the unfarmed countryside, which in the case of Jerusalem was some way outside the city boundary. Immediately around the city were tilled fields, and, of course, the renowned orchards. The procession represents the onset and the course of the Gospel age, the entry into the city still lying some way ahead. We must take special note of the fact that no wedding takes place in this chapter, nor do we even see the procession arrive at the city gates, because this procession is simply another view of the time between the first betrothal (the engagement) and the wedding ceremony. To marry the bride and groom at this stage is a mistake, and one that ruins the point of the poem.

The bride in this procession firstly pictures the church at Pentecost, brought out of the 'wilderness' of the Jewish church. No more would there be the mixed multitude of old Israel, with all the pains due to faithlessness. A new order had arrived in which Christ would be pre-eminent. Also, the Gentiles would be called out of the even wilder wilderness of paganism into the kingdom of Christ. The uncultivated countryside characterised by little food, confusing tracks, wild animals and many dangers, would yield up the bride to her wedding journey.

Secondly, the wedding journey pictures this present Gospel age, and thirdly, the personal spiritual journey of every believer. This is the very journey we are on today, heading for the eternal City, and for the marriage of the Lamb.

Some think the pillars of smoke are incense burning at the head of the procession, but it is more likely (despite the change of metaphor) that these are the enthusiastic rush of smoke associated with newly lit fires, a picture capturing the excitement and anticipation of the church. The perfumes represent the church's God-given graces and marks of salvation (for these are very evident to onlookers), while the powders or ointments brought by travelling merchants suggest the international character of the church.

7 'Behold his bed, which is Solomon's; threescore valiant men are about it, of the valiant of Israel.'

SUDDENLY the maidens or bystanders recognise the carriage of Solomon, exclaiming, 'Look, Solomon's sedan!' (the flexible Hebrew word for bed, in the context of a procession, refers to a carriage). Solomon is the most important of the two parties, and attention quickly focuses upon him. This is not literally Solomon, of course, for he appears in the poem only as a type or symbol of Christ. We see the church here wonderfully blessed, but the most important person is Christ. The sedan or carriage on which Christ travels in the world is none other than His grace and saving work. This is unassailable and undefeatable in the world, for Christ will surely save His elect and bring His purposes to pass – hence the picture of sixty noble defenders encircling the carriage. Some writers also see here pastors and teachers set to defend the faith.

8 'They all hold swords, being expert in war: every man hath his sword upon his thigh because of fear in the night.'

THE WEDDING procession has come a long way, including overnight travel with all its hazards, but its defences ensure that nothing will cause disturbance or delay. Not false religion, empires of unbelief, or all Satan's wiles will prevent the salvation of those who are to be saved. The Truth will prevail.

9 'King Solomon made himself a chariot of the wood of Lebanon.'

THE KINGLY groom made the carriage himself, signifying that Christ made His 'carriage' of grace and salvation (the Gospel) by His atoning death on Calvary. That it was made of wood suggests His condescension in entering into human flesh to die for us.

10 'He made the pillars thereof of silver, the bottom thereof of gold, the covering of it of purple, the midst thereof being paved with love, for the daughters of Jerusalem.'

THE DECORATIONS on the chariot, however, testify to Christ's divine glory and saving accomplishments, and most of all, speak of His love for His children. The silver posts show the *purity and beauty* of the Gospel. In all the world there is no scheme so kind, so life-changing, or so free. The back or base of gold shows the *riches* of the Gospel, for mercy and salvation will embrace the very worst sinners and flow liberally to a vast host of people gathered from every land and every age. To these will be given the priceless blessings of eternal life as co-heirs with the King of kings. The purple fabric of the seats (or curtains) is the colour of *royalty*, and the interior is lined (or fitted) with *love* (the figurative language gives way to the reality) for the daughters, or young converts. Modern versions translate, 'lovingly fitted *by* the daughters of Jerusalem', but we prefer the sense of the *KJV*, 'fitted with his love *for* the daughters'. Thus the carriage of salvation has: (a) purity and beauty; (b) riches; (c) royal stature; and (d) Christ's love for converts.

11 'Go forth, O ye daughters of Zion, and behold king Solomon with the crown wherewith his mother crowned him in the day of his espousals, and in the day of the gladness of his heart.'

THE SPEAKER here is probably the bride, although it could be the bystanders, or even the voice of God. Is this the wedding? No, it is the maidens being urged to look upon the groom wearing the crown or wreath given to him at the initial betrothal some time before. This clearly took place before the bride's exclamation in chapter 2.16, 'My beloved is mine, and I am his.' The maidens are urged to look at the king, the groom, as the one on whom the wedding depended, and we urge new converts and seekers to fix their eyes upon Christ, for He alone is the source of salvation. We say, 'Seek the Lord, repent and believe in Him. Trust Him, love Him, yield to Him, worship Him, for He is your life and your all.'

Christ wears the betrothal crown given, in a sense, by His 'mother', referring to the church, for the church of the Old Testament 'brought forth a man child, who was to rule all nations' *(Revelation 12.5)*, and the church of the New Testament crowned Him as Lord and King. Christ went to Calvary for the joy that was set before Him – the eternal blessedness of His people – and that was the day of His espousal, the first part of the wedding process, the engagement or initial betrothal. Like the maidens, we see our King, and love Him more than we love anything or anyone else.

Once again, a scene closes without a wedding, the recurring riddle of the poem, but this is the point, because the grand wedding will take place at the return of Christ. If this eleventh verse described a wedding, as some suppose, it would amount to the most frugal description of such a day in all literature. What an anticlimax it would be, and how out of character with the rest of the *Song*!

A great hymn of Isaac Watts interprets this eleventh verse in the way we have described, the church's espousal to Christ being the day of Calvary (or from the individual believer's point of view, the time when our hearts truly opened to Calvary), the full wedding not taking place until the Lord's return.

> *Jesus, Thou everlasting King,*
> *Accept the tribute which we bring;*
> *Accept the well-deserved renown,*
> *And wear our praises as Thy crown.*

Let every act of worship be
Like our espousals, Lord, to Thee;
Like the dear hour when from above
We first received Thy pledge of love.

The gladness of that happy day –
Our hearts would wish it long to stay;
Nor let our faith forsake its hold,
Nor comfort sink, nor love grow cold.

Each following minute as it flies,
Increase Thy praise, improve our joys,
Till we are raised to sing Thy name
At the great Supper of the Lamb.

O that the months would roll away,
And bring that coronation day;
The King of Grace shall fill the throne,
His Father's glory all His own.

The Mutual Love of Christ and His People

Christ Describes His Church

1 'Behold, thou art fair, my love; behold, thou art fair; thou hast doves' eyes within thy locks: thy hair is as a flock of goats, that appear from mount Gilead.'

THE GROOM praises his bride, once again using terms which would be inappropriate and even peculiar for human love, but are deeply meaningful if the bride represents the church of Christ. These descriptions of the bride were not designed to vaunt outward, physical beauty, as Matthew Henry points out, 'but the beauty of holiness', or the qualities which Christ gives His people at conversion. Human beings stand back and admire their achievements of craft and creativity, often with unwholesome pride, and Christ also takes delight in His handiwork in the lives of His people but without a trace of sin. He has given believers the graces described in this chapter, and He loves these characteristics. What an incentive it is to us to exercise our graces, when we know that our Saviour loves us for them. How carefully we should honour and preserve them!

The groom's love is mentioned first in the words, 'Thou art fair, my love.' A more modern word would be 'beautiful'. Then he refers to the first grace on the list, the bride's dove-like eyes, alert, observant, docile and non-argumentative toward him (mentioned before). The eyes of believers answer to this, showing eagerness to pick up every morsel of spiritual bread and to enjoy the Word. The eye of the believer is supremely the eye of faith, ready to trust God's way and His promises, and when Christ sees this characteristic in us, He loves us for it.

The bride's eyes are within locks (the Hebrew meaning 'something fastened' or held back), possibly a veil, in which case her modesty is in mind. Humility is certainly a grace given at conversion, seen initially in our humble acceptance of our sin and need, and then in our continuing dependence on Christ, and He loves us for it.

The hair is an ornament of the head, which is the seat of the mind. The bride's hair, intriguingly compared with a dense flock of black goats winding their way down the mountainside, is possibly a figure for the conspicuously well-ordered and principled way of thinking that characterises believers. Some years ago one of the most senior policemen in Britain spoke of how Christian conversion as a young officer had brought him to the Bible, and this had taught him how to think. Prior to this, his thinking processes had been haphazard, but the orderly and interlocking doctrines of the Word, together with the consistent flow of insights into human nature and behaviour, shaped his approach to people, crime, and all other branches of secular life. Christians who grow in grace are conspicuous in society by the thoughtful way they handle life and its problems. This is a very significant grace, and Christ loves to see it. Another suggestion for the meaning of the flock of goats supposes that these were the groom's own goats, in which much wealth was invested. The idea is that Christ cherishes us as a valued possession (made valuable by *grace*). We can understand that Christ should have pity for us, but that He should treasure us is almost beyond our power to grasp.

2 'Thy teeth are like a flock of sheep that are even shorn, which came up from the washing; whereof every one bear twins, and none is barren among them.'

THE BRIDE'S teeth are perfect, but this flattering description clearly alludes to her radiant smile. The groom loves her for her warmth of affection and settled joy. It is evident she is supremely happy to be with him, this being more endearing than the literal perfection of her teeth. Equally, the Lord loves His people for their happiness and appreciation of their benefits, a tendency He gives at conversion. How important it is for us to maintain this grateful joy, keeping our privileges and our future glory constantly before our minds so that we never plunge so low as to lose our happiness in Him. Some believers suffer melancholy (as the Puritans called it) as a mysterious component of their natural temperament, and these words are not intended to discourage such people, but in general Christians should aim at maintaining a joy in the Lord that cannot easily be quenched by burdens, disappointments and cares.

> 'Seven particulars are specified, a number of perfection, for the church is enriched with manifold graces. The images are very bright, the shades strong and the comparisons bold, not fitting to represent external beauty, but the beauty of holiness.'
>
> – Matthew Henry

The use of a perfect flock of sheep as an illustration for teeth leads to another possible lesson, namely that joy (the perfect smile) is associated with humble acceptance of providential circumstances (the habit of sheep). It is usually the case that pride in some form is behind our inability to accept trials and difficulties, leading to the forfeiture of joy.

3 'Thy lips are like a thread of scarlet, and thy speech is comely: thy temples are like a piece of a pomegranate within thy locks.'

THE FIRST part of the verse rather obviously pictures the grace of good speech. At conversion, as part of the new nature, we are given an aptitude for kindness in our words, along with an abhorrence of gossip and backbiting. We also receive a love of spiritual conversation and a desire to witness for Christ. Do we strive to exercise and maintain this gift of good speech, and do we daily repent of any 'unconverted' style of talk? Christ loves to see the graces He has given us valued and kept pure. In prayer this gift of speech is to be manifested in a full range of different kinds of prayer, including praise, love, repentance, dedication and intercession. Impoverished prayer, omitting any of these categories, will not greatly gladden the heart of the Saviour.

The bride's temples suggest dignity and wisdom, adding to the beautiful hair, that ornament of the head, which is the 'palace' of the mind. The groom admires and loves his bride's depth of understanding, insight and discernment. So Christ loves His people when they stir up the gifts He has put within them to become wiser and deeper in their knowledge of His Word, and in the spiritual processing of life's decisions and trials.

4 'Thy neck is like the tower of David builded for an armoury, whereon there hang a thousand bucklers, all shields of mighty men.'

HERE IS another improbable compliment for the groom to pay his bride, because the tower of David was apparently a squat, ungainly structure, more robust than beautiful. (The thousand shields are described as hanging on the outside, whereas literally they were stored inside.) This is obviously a figurative statement illustrating the strength that holds the head erect, unflinchingly facing forward in the midst of troubles. Christ loves His church greatly when her members, each holding firmly their shield of faith, prove Him and stand loyal to the Gospel no matter what may distract or threaten them. Loyalty He prizes highly.

5 'Thy two breasts are like two young roes that are twins, which feed among the lilies.'

NOW THE GROOM, representing our Lord, praises the part of the bride's body nearest to her heart, the symbol of her love. The highest and greatest of all graces given at conversion is love (*1 Corinthians 12.31* and *13.13*). This includes love for God, love for fellow believers, love for the Word, and yearning, sympathetic love for the lost, including the young. When imbued with such broad-spectrum love, the Christian is a delight to the Lord.

Most people possess the capacity to love before conversion, but afterwards their love becomes much more grateful, less selfish, more pure, more sacrificial, and more outward-flowing. If Christ loves our love, let us never allow ourselves to become hardened. Love shed abroad in the heart is not something weak, pathetic or effeminate, but the noblest and strongest grace, and in the *Song* it feeds, like tender roes, among the lilies (representing the church at large), meaning that it thrives best when believers are exercised by and engaged in the worship and labours of God's people.

6 'Until the day break, and the shadows flee away, I will get me to the mountain of myrrh, and to the hill of frankincense.'

WHAT THE BRIDE said in chapter 2 when she pledged her loyalty and called to the groom to return soon, he now echoes, telling her that he must go away until the great day of the wedding. Where will the groom go? Of course, he represents Christ, Who must go to Paradise until His second coming, the time of the bridal supper of the Lamb. The fragrant mountain is inaccessible to us physically, but we may go there now by faith. The sweet smelling groves and woods of frankincense and balsam of the Holy Land represent the place of private prayer and devotion, and also the house of worship and hearing of the Word. Communion by faith is the believer's present privilege and joy until the day when the ultimate delectable mountain comes into full view.

7 'Thou art all fair, my love; there is no spot in thee.'

HERE IS the church's forgiven condition as viewed by the Lord, for He chooses to see us clothed in the garment of His own imputed righteousness. He loves also our *completeness* by grace, for we are somewhat akin to babies born happily with every limb and finger and toe. We may be weak and needy, but viewed spiritually we all possess a measure of every grace. No believer lacks the faculty of prayer, or the capacity for faith, or the new nature. We may in our foolishness not exercise all our graces, but every spiritual birth is a perfect birth and all parts are there. The same applies to any truly believing congregation. All the faculties needed for obedience to Christ and access to blessing are bestowed.

In addition, Christ sees us as spotless by comparison with the world. True believers have been changed and beautified far beyond anything they were as unbelievers, and the Lord loves His handiwork. How carefully we should guard our hearts and keep ourselves unspoiled!

8 'Come with me from Lebanon, my spouse, with me from Lebanon: look from the top of Amana, from the top of Shenir and Hermon, from the lions' dens, from the mountains of the leopards.'

THE GROOM calls to his spouse to leave the barren mountains and follow him to the glorious and beautiful place where he would be. She is to look from her bleak hilltop to the distant landscape, the view ahead, and follow him. Of course, there is great beauty also in the places named, but not for the bride who longs to be where the groom lives. True conversion takes away our taste for the things of this world. She must quit the place of wild beasts and pursue him. So the church surveys the scene ahead, the glories of a walk with Christ and the future glory, and leaves worldly goals and ways to take the heavenward road. There is no middle way in the Christian life, for we either remain as worldlings, or we launch out as children of Heaven, but we cannot have a foot in each place. Lions and leopards in the form of Satan and his host will tear our soul and character if we compromise and remain as worldly Christians. Watts penned the lines –

> He calls me from the leopard's den,
> From this wide world of beasts and men,
> To Zion, where His glories are;
> Not Lebanon is half so fair.
>
> Nor dens of prey, nor flowery plains,
> Nor earthly joys, nor earthly pains,
> Shall hold my feet or force my stay,
> When Christ invites my soul away.

9 'Thou hast ravished my heart, my sister, my spouse; thou hast ravished my heart with one of thine eyes, with one chain of thy neck.'

'RAVISHED' here means something like 'taken away' or 'captured'. Yet again we are to note how greatly Christ loves us. His is not just protective love, glorious as this is, but a love of deep affection and delight. We repeat, it is hard for us to take this in, that the mighty Maker of all loves us with the fondness and intensity of a groom for a bride. Says Cowper –

> Lord, it is my chief complaint
> That my love is weak and faint.

So it is, and we should be burdened to reflect more upon our Lord's lovingkindness, to praise Him more, and to curb our excessive love for those things in this world which steal away the affection that belongs to Him. Let us remember that our Lord ever intercedes for us. Let us be moved to think that He will be present at our every sickbed, at hand in all our troubles and triumphs, and with us in the moment of death, in order to exercise His great love for us. He has every believer on His heart and His joy is in our spiritual advance. We may tell Him anything, and He will hear with immeasurable and everlasting love, because (astonishing thought) we have captured His heart and, according to this verse, we have done so with only two of the many graces He has given us.

10 'How fair is thy love, my sister, my spouse! how much better is thy love than wine! and the smell of thine ointments than all spices!'

THE GROOM now repeats to the bride that he *loves her love*. This is not about her physical beauty, but her love to him. So Christ loves our love, and therefore we should express this in words and also do all the things that express love. We should study Him, speak to Him often, look forward to being with Him, represent Him, work for His cause, defend His name, reflect on His wonders, and so *love* Him. Let the heart be tender and moveable whenever He is in mind, and love Him as the One vastly greater in our esteem than all the famous names of this world put together.

11 'Thy lips, O my spouse, drop as the honeycomb: honey and milk are under thy tongue; and the smell of thy garments is like the smell of Lebanon.'

THE GROOM here goes further than praising the *character* of the bride's words to say how sweet and acceptable they are to him. Yet again we are moved and amazed to think that the Lord of Heaven and earth derives great pleasure from hearing our feeble words, whether expressing praise and worship to Him, or speaking words of compassion, edification and comfort to others. And how pleased He is also to hear our words of witness representing Him to lost souls around us!

12 'A garden inclosed is my sister, my spouse; a spring shut up, a fountain sealed.'

NOW THE great garden metaphor begins in which the bride is herself described in terms of a delightful walled garden for the pleasure of the groom. She is designed and kept for him to visit, and how well this describes the character and purpose of the church, or of any saved individual. As a walled garden a true congregation (or an individual believer) is distinctive and set apart from the world and sin to be for Christ. Here, a great variety of beautiful plants grow and flower, illustrating all the spiritual graces and character graces given by the Lord. These, of course, must be cultivated and the ground dug and weeded, otherwise the thorns and briars of misconduct and backsliding will invade and conquer. Christian sanctification is in mind.

The plants are attractively ordered, picturing the well-sanctified believer's organised, faithful adherence to spiritual duties and commitments.

'This relationship amounts to unity, insomuch that the spouse loses her name, loses her identity, and, to a high degree, is merged in the greater personality to which she is united. Such is our union to Christ. He loves us so much that He has taken us up into Himself by the absorption of love.'

– C. H. Spurgeon

The privacy of this special garden reflects the practice of personal communion with Christ, while the spring or fountain suggests the energising and sustaining power and joy provided by the Holy Spirit – a well of water springing up into eternal life. The spring is barred or sealed from the interference of any who might pollute, destroy or steal from it, illustrating the security of a believer's spiritual life. And just as the individual is comforted by the doctrine of final perseverance, so a *faithful* congregation may be sure that the gates of hell shall not prevail against it, so that its witness will prevail from generation to generation. Watts writes of the church –

We are a garden walled around,
Chosen and made peculiar ground;
A little spot enclosed by grace
Out of the world's wide wilderness.

13 'Thy plants are an orchard of pomegranates, with pleasant fruits; camphire, with spikenard,

14 'Spikenard and saffron; calamus and cinnamon, with all trees of frankincense; myrrh and aloes, with all the chief spices.'

THE GROOM continues to list the bride's graces, referring particularly to fruitbearing and scented plants, indicating that congregations and individual believers are equipped to be *useful* to the Lord Who loves them for their fruits of character and soulwinning. Certainly, these fruits come only by His generous power and blessing, yet He loves His people as if they had achieved them by their own effort. We are converted not only that we might believe and love Him, but also that we might bear fruit, and permeate society with the aroma of the knowledge of God.

The plants named, experts tell us, do not generally grow in the wilderness, but only in fertile and cultivated places, showing that the graces they represent are best found in believers. (It should convict us that these graces are sometimes stronger in wordlings than in ourselves.) Some are evergreen, denoting that spiritual joy and peace can flourish even in the winter storms of life. All possess medicinal properties, indicating that, alongside the fruits and scents of character and Gospel influence, believers should be beneficial in the world through compassionate and helpful acts. Myrrh and aloes also have preservative properties (including the embalming of bodies), suggesting the peace-making role of God's children (mentioned in the Sermon on the Mount), and also their influence in preserving a measure of morality and dignity in a decadent society. The Lord loves His church for this.

15 'A fountain of gardens, a well of living waters, and streams from Lebanon.'

THESE WORDS could be those of the groom to the bride, or hers to him. It may be that the bride, having been praised, turns that praise back to her kingly groom saying, in effect, 'But *you* are the fountain of many gardens...' This would certainly fit the glorious work of Christ through the Gospel, for from Him flows an abundant, unfailing stream of justifying grace, wisdom, peace, assurance, and strength to needy souls.

If, however, they are the groom's words, then the bride is praised in figurative language for being a benefactor and blessing to others, and this is, or should be, true of the church. Like streams from the mountain ranges of Lebanon that water the plains, so Gospel witness goes forth from the people of God to bring conversion and blessing to countless lost people. Does this describe our church and our individual lives?

16 'Awake, O north wind; and come, thou south; blow upon my garden, that the spices thereof may flow out. Let my beloved come into his garden, and eat his pleasant fruits.'

THIS VERSE – or the first half of it – must be the groom speaking, because only Christ can command the winds to blow. Without doubt, the winds here represent the trials of life. The purpose of these trials is that the fragrance of the garden may flow out, witnessing to those around us of the character of our renewed lives. In our family circle, or our place of study or work, it will be seen that we are different people, and that we have a firm hold on divine resources. The spices are patience, prayerfulness, joy, peace and a well-controlled temperament. The north and south winds conflict, producing unpredictable events occurring with variable strength, but through them all we are refined, drawn nearer to the Lord, and thus given a firm 'platform' of character from which to witness.

In the second half of the verse the bride speaks, asking the groom to come into the garden of her life, because if he is with her when these storms arise all will be well. So too we pray to Christ to be with us by His Spirit, giving light on the Word and strength to stand. We ask for assurance, calm deportment, warm faith, much help, and an opportunity to represent Him in all the circumstances of life. 'Come Lord,' we say, 'and let us bear fruit for Thee.' This prayer is the substance of these verses by Isaac Watts –

> *Awake, O heavenly wind! and come,*
> *Blow on this garden of perfume;*
> *Spirit divine! descend and breathe*
> *A gracious gale on plants beneath.*
>
> *Make our best spices flow abroad,*
> *To entertain our Saviour God;*
> *And faith, and love, and joy appear,*
> *And every grace be active here.*

The Mutual Love of Christ and His People

A Healing View of Christ

1 'I am come into my garden, my sister, my spouse: I have gathered my myrrh with my spice; I have eaten my honeycomb with my honey; I have drunk my wine with my milk: eat, O friends; drink, yea, drink abundantly, O beloved.'

NO SOONER has the bride called to him than the groom enters the garden, bringing all that is needed for a banquet. Christ also hears us, graciously accepts our worship, and the feeble effort we make to serve and please Him (our 'myrrh and spices') and gives our souls, through His Word, a feast of good things. This pictures an elevated time of communion with Christ. The serving church is especially blessed, together with all her young converts and seekers (the 'friends' or maidens-in-waiting). The words 'sister' and 'spouse' used together provide a powerful expression of Christ's loving union with His people.

2 'I sleep, but my heart waketh: it is the voice of my beloved that knocketh, saying, Open to me, my sister, my love, my dove, my undefiled: for my head is filled with dew, and my locks with the drops of the night.'

THIS IS where the fifth chapter ought to begin, for here the scene changes, and the bride recounts to her maidens her sad experience, perhaps following the banquet of blessing. This is not a 'bedroom scene', depicting the quarrel of a fully married couple, but is about the visit of an 'engaged' groom to his bride-to-be and her reluctance to rise, dress and receive him. She is in her house half-asleep and half-awake, and here we can imagine ourselves as a church or as individual believers in this very condition, spiritually. We are not necessarily in a backslidden or wilfully disobedient state, but we are not alert, engaged, enthusiastic, and feelingful as we ought to be. We hear the voice of Christ in His Word, but we are not responsive. Services are held, a full church programme is maintained, and personal devotions are kept up, but self-examination has become infrequent, and reflection on the things of Christ rare. Praise has become half-hearted, and prayers mechanical, to the extent that spiritual duties sometimes seem inconvenient. This is the sad and low condition depicted by the half-asleep bride: a drowsy, self-preoccupied state in which Christ is taken for granted.

In a sleepy condition like this a church soon drops its guard, allows evangelistic efforts to fade, slides into worldliness, and succumbs to internal troubles. A spiritually sleepy believer takes more leisure and pleasure, turning increasingly to secular concerns, and looking to possessions and career advance to satisfy the longings of the heart. It has been said that the sleeping aspect illustrates the old nature, and the waking the new, and these now share authority in the believer's life. Where this is the case, the old nature soon dominates.

At this point the bride hears the voice of the groom calling from outside her door. He knocks and appeals to her with various expressions of endearment. This is how Christ calls to us when we are half-awake as Christians, perhaps through friends, or through the Word, or by a direct touch upon the conscience, or by the agency of troubles and heartache. It is the call of *Revelation 3.20*:

> 'Behold, I stand at the door, and knock: if any man hear my voice, and open the door, I will come in to him, and will sup with him, and he with me.'

'Open to Me!' He calls, 'Honour Me and return to My full authority. Listen to Me. Love Me more than yourself and the things of the world.' In the poem, the groom uses several titles of endearment showing that his rousing call is for the good of the bride, who is greatly loved.

The groom goes on to say that his head (his hair) is wet with the dew and the rain, not in an appeal for pity, but to show the bride how much he must love her to visit her in such unpleasant conditions. When Christ calls us to greater commitment, we should be reminded of the lengths to which He has gone for us, the humiliation He has endured for us, and the pain He has borne to save us. We should also think of the punishment He suffered for our present state of apathy and disobedience, for this must surely move us.

3 'I have put off my coat; how shall I put it on? I have washed my feet; how shall I defile them?'

THE BRIDE, however, is hard of heart and foolish. To respond is all too much trouble. 'Why should I dress again?' she asks. She has succumbed to ease, and is now reluctant, recalcitrant and grudging, and so are we in the equivalent spiritual condition. Christ is lowered in our estimation. We have put off the coat of reliance on Him, and washed our feet from His service. There was a time when we would have done anything for Him and done it gladly and immediately for nothing was too much. We were like the young men in World War II who volunteered in their hundreds of thousands to defend their land, even though it could cost life or limb. But with us, that level of commitment and earnestness has disappeared. What an unthinkable way to treat Christ when we largely shut Him out of our concerns.

4 'My beloved put in his hand by the hole of the door, and my bowels were moved for him.'

THE HOLE in the door[*] may have been a shielded aperture provided to reach a latch. As the groom's hand appeared, the bride's heart melted and her love was kindled. When we are half awake, Christ may similarly move us by jolting the conscience, touching the heart, stirring the feelings, and bringing conviction and alarm to our souls.

5 'I rose up to open to my beloved; and my hands dropped with myrrh, and my fingers with sweet smelling myrrh, upon the handles of the lock.

6 'I opened to my beloved; but my beloved had withdrawn himself, and was gone: my soul failed when he spake: I sought him, but I could not find him; I called him, but he gave me no answer.'

THE BRIDE now rises and takes hold of the latch, her fingers full of love and desire, but the groom has gone. We shake ourselves out of our spiritual lethargy and take hold of the latch of prayer, our hands dripping with both faith and longing for a fresh engagement with Christ, but He is not there. We have left it too long and He has withdrawn from us. That precious sense of certainty that God hears, fails us. Answers to prayer cease, strength subsides, and joy in the Word cannot be revived, because we must now be chastised for our ingratitude, lack of love, lightness, pride, self-concern, love of ease, and indifference to the voice of conscience. The painfulness of the bride's loss when she cannot find her groom is seen in her

[*] 'Door' assumed, but not in the Hebrew.

repeated dismay, which we may paraphrase: 'He is gone! He is gone!' Is this sometimes our penalty for coldness?

7 'The watchmen that went about the city found me, they smote me, they wounded me; the keepers of the walls took away my veil from me.'

WHEN WE first met the watchmen in chapter three, we identified them as the church's pastors, but here we see them engaged in cruelty, attacking the bride and taking away the veil or garment that possibly marked her out as a betrothed woman. But in the licence of an allegory the harsh treatment is her perception rather than the reality. When we are disobedient and sink to a very low spiritual state even the kind words of Scripture often make us feel worse. Every verse seems to condemn us, taking away our 'veil' or sense of belonging to Christ. Ease and lightness in believers (and in churches) can lead to such a 'night' of spiritual loneliness and near despair.

8 'I charge you, O daughters of Jerusalem, if ye find my beloved, that ye tell him, that I am sick of love.'

THE BRIDE appeals to the maidens to find her groom and tell him she is faint with the love she has for him, this scene picturing the discouraging effect the low state of a church has on young believers or seekers. Those who have been helped by us are now dismayed to see our doubt and confusion. Those we have spiritually 'parented' or nurtured are pained by our condition.

9 'What is thy beloved more than another beloved, O thou fairest among women? what is thy beloved more than another beloved, that thou dost so charge us?'

THE RESPONSE of the maidens is to doubt the glories of the groom, saying, in effect, 'What is so wonderful in him that you yearn so much to see him?' To be fair, they may mean their question in a more positive way, saying, 'Tell us what is so wonderful about your beloved, that we may value him also.' What follows is a golden treasury of spiritual counsel for a wayward and sad soul (or congregation). The bride considers and proclaims with all her heart the exceptional attributes and ways of her beloved, and this will shortly bring her to him. Similarly the way back to Christ for the languishing believer is to reflect on Him; to appreciate Him; to value Him above all else; to long for Him; and so to love Him. The succeeding verses show the way back to assurance and blessing.

What could Old Testament believers have known about the coming Christ? A great deal, from this allegorical description given by the bride. Do we know *more* with New Testament light? We certainly know more about Christ's *work*, but if we desire to 'see' His person, the *Song* tells us as much as we may know this side of eternity. This glorious passage is one of the very brightest jewels in the entire Bible, and when young believers and seekers of our day (not to mention ourselves) ask, 'What is thy beloved?' this is a description to overwhelm the soul.

Significantly, only three components in this description refer to his physical appearance, while nine components are likened to materials unconnected with the human body. The text virtually calls out to us saying, 'Don't take this as a description of physical beauty, but of character and spiritual graces.'

10 'My beloved is white and ruddy, the chiefest among ten thousand.'

THIS HAS nothing to do with ethnicity, the word 'white' being an inappropriate translation of the Hebrew *dazzling*. 'My beloved is radiant' would be better, or 'bright as dazzling white light'. This refers to a man far, far higher than any ordinary person. His sublime holiness is being described, along with His divine nature, power and glory. He will come as a human being, because the description gives Him human features, but His divinity will shine through (as at the transfiguration). The *spiritual* brightness emanating from Him will light up this dark world with saving grace, imparting itself to individuals, giving life and happiness. As the only radiant One, He will be conspicuous and outstanding in world history, overcoming darkness at Calvary. And when He returns in power and glory the brightness of His coming will destroy the power of evil and bring in the dawn of eternal glory.

He is also 'ruddy', or flushed with health and vigour, distinguishing Him from a feeble, lethargic person. He will zealously and effectively work righteousness for us and accomplish salvation. He is the chief among ten thousand, being more important and significant than all angels, prophets, and priests put together, and also far greater than the most renowned names of human achievement and power. He has accomplished the supreme deed and the greatest transaction by the purchase of souls on Calvary, and He alone sustains the world

> 'He is *the chief among ten thousand*, fairer than the children of men, than any of them, than all of them, there is none like Him, everything else is to be accounted loss and dung in comparison with Him; for He is higher than … any of the principalities and powers of the upper or lower world.'
>
> – Matthew Henry

and holds back the final curtain of judgement. He is the outstanding One in personal qualities, in unselfishness, in kindness, in love, in approachability, and in terms of every noble standard.

The Hebrew for 'chiefest' may also be rendered 'standard-bearer'. Older commentators used to enjoy explaining this sense, saying, 'He carries the standard for us.' The old-time standard-bearer in an army had to be exceptionally strong and able, because the streaming standard represented the success of the entire brigade. So Christ became the representative of the human race, deserving Heaven for us, and atoning for our sin. 'He bore our curse,' said a Puritan, 'and we bear His name.' He is the supreme standard-bearer.

11 'His head is as the most fine gold, his locks are bushy, and black as a raven.'

THE GROOM'S head is at first sight described in a contradictory way, for it is first gold, and then black. Clearly, it is not the colour of either hair or face that is in mind, but the *material* of which it is composed. His value and status is so high that His head is of the very finest, purest gold. Once again, His divinity is in mind, particularly His imperishability and His flawless holiness. The head is the location of wisdom, and His wisdom is infinite, eternal and priceless. To have Christ is to have the greatest possible riches, and if we value Him, we shall surrender everything for Him. Said Paul:

> 'Yea doubtless, and I count all things but loss for the excellency of the knowledge of Christ Jesus my Lord: for whom I have suffered the loss of all things, and do count them but dung, that I may win Christ' *(Philippians 3.8)*.

What more could we possess than the Saviour of the world, our Friend in Heaven, our perfect Guide, our all-knowing Teacher, our gracious Sanctifier, our Lord and the ultimate 'Hero'? He is our 'exceeding great reward' – why should we ever pine for mere earthly things?

The groom's bushy, black locks possibly portray our Lord's eternal youth, complementing the white hair of the Ancient of Days in *Daniel* and *Revelation*. The latter speaks of His unfailing wisdom, the former of inextinguishable power and vigour. He will never age or fade as earthly emperors do for He possesses eternal 'youth', ever living to make intercession for and to bless His people.

Just as the bride's hair (earlier) was an ornament of her head representing her well-ordered thinking, so the groom's jet black hair suggests Christ's deep and mysterious will. How comforting it is when storm-tossed to know that He has a perfect plan for us. Whether He is chastening or training us up through difficulties, we know His will is perfect, and all will ultimately be made clear.

12 'His eyes are as the eyes of doves by the rivers of waters, washed with milk, and fitly set.'

OUR TRANSLATION, in trying to help us, has inserted italicised words which tend to confuse and spoil the sense. In the first chapter the bride's eyes were like the eyes of doves, but here the groom's eyes *are* doves – according to the literal Hebrew. Messiah's eyes may be likened to beautiful white doves bathing at the riverside *in milk* to accentuate their whiteness. The meaning is that Christ's view is pure, knowing no lust, no jealousy, and no vindictiveness. When He looks upon His people, He delights in genuineness and godliness.

His eyes are also 'fitly set', or 'fitly placed and set as a precious stone in the foil or reflective mounting of a ring'. This may be a way of saying that nothing is hidden from His view, but, better, it may refer to a great warmth, even a kindly twinkle, in His eye. He is Creator and Judge of all, but what gentleness and affection He has for His people! One day we shall be amazed at that look!

13 'His cheeks are as a bed of spices, as sweet flowers: his lips like lilies, dropping sweet smelling myrrh.'

'HIS CHEEKS' represent the recognisable part of the groom's face – his distinctive features. When Messiah came His most recognisable features were His lovingkindness, His mercy, His grace, His teaching and His power. The blissful news of free forgiveness, restoration and communion was the aroma of flowers and balsam by which He was desired and remembered by His disciples. When He comes the second time, we too will be overwhelmed by His gracious character. No doubt His literal appearance will seize all our powers of comprehension and wonder, but His divine mercy and redeeming love will register with equal power. We see Him now, by faith, at Calvary, and we also recognise Him everywhere in the pages of the Bible. But soon we shall see Him face to face and then we shall be lost in joy unspeakable and full of glory.

His lips or His words drop sweet-smelling spices, literally forgiving words, promises, and assurances. Let us pray to hear and feel the encouraging words of Christ every time we read Scripture, and so appreciate Him more and more.

14 'His hands are as gold rings set with the beryl: his belly is as bright ivory overlaid with sapphires.'

THE 'RINGS' here (the Hebrew means something round or folded) are nowadays translated 'rods', as if describing fingers of gold. The verse best refers to the *open*, extended hand of action, its fingers being adorned by rings of beryl (or olivine), transparent and green. This represents the perfect work of Christ, as described in *Isaiah 40.10*, 'Behold, the Lord God will come with strong hand, and his arm shall rule for him.' What He does will fulfil the plan of salvation, with eternal results. The gemstones of fruitfulness and peace picture well the purpose of His coming. This is picture-language which would have been meaningful in the culture of Old Testament Jews, prophesying the reconciling mission of Messiah.

'His belly' (modern translations say body or abdomen) is actually the same Hebrew word translated 'bowels' in verse 4. This soft part of the abdomen – the bowels – is the Hebrew way of speaking about a person's innermost feelings of, say, love, compassion, or desire, and this is plainly the sense here. When Messiah comes He will be seen to have a deep affection for His people that will never be diminished. His feelings, though tender, are as strong and durable as ivory. They will take Him to Calvary, through indescribable agonies, and on into glory to be our Lord for ever.

Entirely overlaid with blue sapphire, the affection of Christ is flawless and breathtaking. How greatly we must love Him and how willingly we must yield to Him, as churches and as people! So the bride extols her groom.

15 'His legs are as pillars of marble, set upon sockets of fine gold: his countenance is as Lebanon, excellent as the cedars.'

IN MAKING her word-portrait of her groom, the bride sees not legs, but massive columns of marble capable of supporting a tremendous load. These describe the strength of Christ in carrying out His purposes and supporting His people. He successfully bore the load of human sin until full atonement was achieved for all His people. He upholds the universe by His word of power, maintaining a material world through both time and eternity. He keeps His people, so that there will always be a church giving light to the world and gathering in the elect until the very last day.

These marble pillars have pure gold sockets or bases, indicating that the foundations are imperishable and precious. The foundations of the faith are the proclamation of God's holiness, man's need, and Christ's redemptive work. These and other fundamental truths must always be at the forefront of all preaching and worship. A 'systematic' and thorough knowledge of Christian doctrine is essential for all believers, for it is the neglect of this that opens the door to false doctrine, leaving believers an easy prey to unbalanced and unfruitful spiritual lives.

'His countenance', referring to Christ's general appearance and disposition, is like a great forest of tall cedars in Lebanon, a picture which would have conveyed to ancient readers Messiah's stateliness, power, abundance, beauty and fragrant character. Cut down one tree, and there are tens of thousands more. Nothing will ever diminish the infinite and eternal Son of God.

16 'His mouth is most sweet: yea, he is altogether lovely. This is my beloved, and this is my friend, O daughters of Jerusalem.'

CHRIST'S WORD is life and health and wonder to us. It brings us to justification, adoption and glory, holds our souls day by day, sweetens all our distresses, and keeps our Lord before our eyes.

The moment we fail to resort to the Word in trouble, we succumb to self-pity and lose the best of our peace.

As the years go by we increasingly cherish the psalms as well as all the other profound and uplifting passages, and most of all when they lead us to see Christ and His ways.

The Lord is 'altogether lovely' in the sense that He is 'altogether desirable', an alternative rendering. The bride has been without her groom for a while, and it has shaken her, broken her complacency and stirred her reflections. How often we pass through the same experience, and then, when we think more worthily of the Lord, His work and His amazing patience with us, we are lost in wonder and praise. Is there another chapter in the Bible to be compared with this portrait of our Saviour?

'I have described him to you,' says the bride with touching simplicity to the maidens-in-waiting. 'This is my beloved,' she murmurs, and then (with the emphasis on the *my*) – 'This is *my* friend.'

To describe Christ, our Friend, to others and especially to encourage seekers and young believers with our testimony, is a primary duty and pleasure for established Christians, yet sometimes it seems as if the longer we have known Him the less we say about Him, and this is clearly a terrible fault. It is frequently necessary to give advanced counsel and teaching to others, but we should all strive to give more personal testimony in the style of the bride – 'This is my beloved, and this is my friend.' She may serve as a model for us all as we represent Him through individual witness.

The inspired writer of the *Song* is compelled to convey this elevated, rhapsodic vision of Christ within the limits of earthly pictures, but what will it really be like when we see Christ through death or His coming? We know we shall see far more than the language of Solomon's love poem can express. This is incomprehensible ground to us now, but in the light of this chapter we may speculate a little on the effect of that coming meeting with the

Lord. As He is the sum total of everything to be desired, and the assembled aggregate of every beautiful object in the bride's description, we may glean the following.

To see Him will have an impact upon us similar to seeing and sensing all the most spectacular and precious sights and experiences added together. We may think of the most wonderful feeling of relief and gratitude we have ever experienced, when perhaps some terrible fear was removed. We may add to this the deepest sensation of love we have ever felt, and also the most humbling sense of awe and wonder. Then we may add the greatest surge of excitement we have ever encountered, along with the most powerful thrill of triumph that ever swept over us. Finally we may combine with all these the most profound amazement at breathtaking scenes of beauty and power that we have ever experienced. If we take all these magnificent impressions together, the very best of earthly sensations, magnified many times, we will have some small sense of the majesty and wonder of seeing Christ Jesus our Lord.

The Mutual Love of Christ and His People

Love for a Militant Church

1 'Whither is thy beloved gone, O thou fairest among women? whither is thy
beloved turned aside? that we may seek him with thee.'

THE BRIDE-TO-BE has temporarily lost contact with her groom
just as believers sometimes lose their footing in the spiritual
life, along with their assurance, and, like the bride, seek to regain the
presence of the Lord. This bride has enlisted the help of the maidens
to find her groom, which means she has shared her woe with those
to whom she was normally guide and teacher. Naturally, they want
to know why she has lost contact, and how he may be found. Of
course, they want to find him and know him also. These maidens
represent seekers and young converts who have seen through this
present world, realising that all is futility without Christ. Now they
seem to teach the bride a lesson, virtually saying, 'But why should

such a friend as the glorious person you have described to us turn away from you, even for a time? Surely, he would not be unfaithful to you? You must know where he will be.'

The question is important for us. Why should Christ ever withdraw from us? The first matter we should consider is the possibility that we have driven Him away by our sin, perhaps of disobedience, or foolishness, or worldliness, and for such things we need to repent. It is noteworthy that the maidens do not think the groom has gone, but only 'turned aside', which is a temporary matter.

> '*O thou fairest among women*, say the maidens to the bride, following her description of the groom. As our knowledge of Christ and our love to Him increase, so do our love unto and esteem for His people.'
>
> – John Gill

The bride, however, has already realised where her groom will be. No doubt her rehearsal of his virtues has spoken to her own heart, and she has realised afresh his faithfulness and his characteristic ways. If we should experience spiritually dark hours, we too will soon remember Christ's faithfulness and the 'place' where we can re-engage Him, through reflection and praise.

2 'My beloved is gone down into his garden, to the beds of spices, to feed in the gardens, and to gather lilies.'

SO THE BRIDE now describes where the groom may be found. The garden, which we were introduced to in chapter 4, is another picture of the church, or more precisely a picture of the place where the church engages in prayer and communion with Christ. In other words, Christ is where He may be found by prayer. Why did this not occur to the bride before? Often, it does not seem to occur to us when we are swept away by trying events, unspiritual objectives, or loss of assurance. The spices of the garden plainly represent Christian graces, especially when exercised in devotions and worship, graces such as light and understanding, faith and assurance.

The bride interestingly says that the groom has gone into the garden 'to feed'. Of course, it is we who are fed by Him. The language suggests a shepherd providing for the sheep, except that we, the sheep, are not fed in the fields but through a banquet in a garden, an encouraging mixing of metaphors. Christ also gathers lilies, which represent our praises and love.

3 'I am my beloved's, and my beloved is mine: he feedeth among the lilies.'

WE NOTICE that this affirmation of faith is expressed the opposite way round from that in chapter 2 verse 16, where it is 'My beloved is mine, and I am his.' This earlier profession is spurred by wonder and amazement at the thought that such a groom is hers. The latter profession seems to be spurred by a strong sense of obligation, putting first 'I am his.' It has been said that one of the greatest lessons in the Christian life is to learn to say, 'I am not my own,' and this is true. When we come to the point that we really feel this, we have made some progress. We say with the bride, 'I am the Lord's; I belong to Him. I must clear everything I do with Him and seek His guidance, for He must come first in all things.'

The bride has moved from wonder to servanthood, and brought herself under the government of her king and shepherd. Philip Doddridge's words flow from this verse:

> 'Tis done! the great transaction's done;
> I am my Lord's, and He is mine;
> He drew me, and I followed on,
> Charmed to confess the voice divine.

George W. Robinson's hymn also captures the sense:

> Loved with everlasting love,
> Led by grace that love to know,
> Spirit, breathing from above,
> Thou hast taught me it is so.

O this full and perfect peace!
O this transport all divine!
In a love which cannot cease,
I am His, and He is mine.

4 'Thou art beautiful, O my love, as Tirzah, comely as Jerusalem, terrible as an army with banners.'

NO SOONER has the bride heard these words than the groom responds to her, assuring her of his love with new descriptions of her virtues (and some used previously in chapters 4 and 5, but now put in a fresh context). The bride is as beautiful as Tirzah, a place in old Palestine, although the meaning of the name is probably in mind, which is – full of delight, or very grateful and appreciative. The church is beautiful to Christ when she is humbly grateful and more than satisfied with God's grace and providential care. Gratitude is the first beautiful feature named by the Lord.

The second beautiful feature is derived from the comeliness of Jerusalem, which was her magnificent Temple, the largest sacred compound in the ancient world, dominating the cultural life of the city. This clearly represents the orderliness of the church (or the individual believer) having Christ and His worship and service as the chief and organising principle of life. Christ loves us when we so order our lives as to keep our devotional times and our church service opportunities well guarded, and when all our major decisions are all taken in the light of His glory.

The third beautiful feature, so loved by the Lord, is our ready militancy to hold the Gospel cause before the world. Here is the 'church militant' with its banners held aloft, not the doctrinally sound but half asleep church (or individual) unconcerned about His glory or about souls dying. The same militant determination is also directed against personal sin. 'Blessed are they which do hunger and thirst after righteousness,' said the Lord, 'for they shall be filled.' The witnessing militancy of believers colours this whole chapter, being mentioned again in verses 10 and 12.

5 'Turn away thine eyes from me, for they have overcome me: thy hair is as a flock of goats that appear from Gilead.

6 'Thy teeth are as a flock of sheep which go up from the washing, whereof every one beareth twins, and there is not one barren among them.

7 'As a piece of a pomegranate are thy temples within thy locks.'

OUR TRANSLATORS have the groom saying, 'Look away from me, for your eyes have conquered me.' An equally valid translation (which this writer prefers) is, 'Turn about your eyes!' The two have been parted, but now the bride returns to the garden and the groom graciously says, in effect, 'Look to me again, and depend on me, for your humble, appreciative, obedient look moves my heart.'

At this point the bride's virtues are repeated, her flowing hair (4.1), her teeth (4.2), and her temples (4.3), referring to her distinctive way of thinking matters out, her radiant smile, and her dignity and wisdom. We believe these are mentioned again as the subject is now the militant or witnessing church, and these features must be applied to this. Thus the ideal church automatically thinks about her witness opportunities in every situation, maintaining her winsomeness before a watching and often hostile world. So, of course, do individual believers, and Christ loves us when our testimony is ever in our mind and governing our deportment, because this is something for Him. Having explained the details of these features already, we will move directly to verse 8.

8 'There are threescore queens, and fourscore concubines, and virgins without number.'

WHAT AN INTRIGUING verse! We cannot see any significance in the numbers but they present a powerful scene to the imagination. (We remember that this is a poem.) Numerous queens and concubines and innumerable unmarried young ladies are here, and the point is made in verse 9.

9 'My dove, my undefiled is but one; she is the only one of her mother, she is the choice one of her that bare her. The daughters saw her, and blessed her; yea, the queens and the concubines, and they praised her.'

THE GROOM says something like this: 'You may assemble all the queens in the world together with all the concubines of their polygamous kings and all their unmarried daughters, but their combined beauty will not match the excellencies of my bride, who they will praise.' The church, in other words, is prized by Christ far above every vaunted person and institution of this world. To Christ, the church is like an only child on whom all parental hopes and affections are fixed. A great host of people from every kingdom will see the happiness and godliness of believers and admit that the church of Christ is the most privileged company in the world. Then they will seek her Lord. Remember, this block of verses is about the witnessing church – a light set upon a hill – and so the praise of the queens suggests the calling of the Gentiles and the great missionary movement.

10 'Who is she that looketh forth as the morning, fair as the moon, clear as the sun, and terrible as an army with banners?'

THIS VERSE is probably uttered by the daughters of Jerusalem, although it could be unidentified bystanders. They are talking about the bride, who resembles the rising dawn when the 'roseate hues' increasingly spread across the landscape. Who is this? It is, of course, a picture of the growing church of Christ from which Gospel truth – marvellous to the saved and uncontaminated as the sun – streams forth. She is the church militant with her banners. An unevangelistic local congregation is hardly an object of the Saviour's special love.

11 'I went down into the garden of nuts to see the fruits of the valley, and to see whether the vine flourished, and the pomegranates budded.'

IN VERSE 2 the bride suddenly remembered that her groom was in the garden of prayer, and in this verse he tells her why he was there. Christ is always with His church, waiting at the prescribed meeting place for the return of His people from waywardness or coolness of spirit. There He observes the progress of the fruits of the valley. Are we exercising the graces He has given to us? Are we providing spiritual fruit of righteousness and of souls saved? His eye is ever upon us. Isaac Watts maintains a kind of running commentary on these verses in his hymn based on the *Song*:

> *My best-belovèd keeps His throne*
> *On hills of light, in worlds unknown;*
> *But He descends and shows His face*
> *In the fair gardens of His grace.*
>
> *He has engrossed my warmest love;*
> *No earthly charms my soul can move:*
> *I have a mansion in His heart,*
> *Nor death nor hell shall make us part.*

12 'Or ever I was aware, my soul made me like the chariots of Amminadib.'

LITERALLY the groom says, 'I knew not,' but our translators have caught the intended sense – 'Before I knew it . . . ' Suddenly the groom's soul set him on or over chariots (the sense of the Hebrew). To whom did these chariots belong? The *KJV* says – Amminadib, for that is the Hebrew word. But the alternative translation, and this is surely right, gives the *meaning* of the word, saying they were the chariots of 'my noble (or willing) people'. So Christ effectively says, 'I go to look at the graces of My church and to observe progress, and when I see My people returning to Me from waywardness, and giving themselves to willing service, I am moved to empower them, bless them, and lead them in the spiritual battle for the Truth, and for souls.' Watts provides two powerful stanzas:

> *He lifts my soul ere I'm aware,*
> *And shows me where His glories are:*
> *No earthly poet, sage or scribe*
> *This heavenly rapture could describe.*
>
> *O, may my spirit daily rise*
> *On wings of faith above the skies,*
> *Till death shall seal my last remove,*
> *To dwell for ever with my Love.*

13 'Return, return, O Shulamite; return, return, that we may look upon thee. What will ye see in the Shulamite? As it were the company of two armies.'

FINALLY in this chapter the groom calls to the bride. Some think the daughters of Jerusalem make this appeal, but we think this verse is all the groom speaking. 'Shulamite' could refer to her as a woman of Shunem (near Mount Gilboa), perhaps reminding her that she had been brought from a lowly, provincial station. Equally 'Shulamite' could be a feminine form of Solomon, which would be a way of saying she was a queen in the groom's eyes. The latter would be nice, but we think the gentle tones of the Lord calling wayward or lazy believers back to His service is the correct sense. 'Shulamite' then reminds them of their origins, to show that He has called them out of the past, and wants them to grow in dedication and grace.

'What will be seen in the bride?' asks the groom, when she returns. How will she be regarded by him? The curious answer is – as two armies; a double camp. Modern translations see two dancing companies here, but they are inclined to introduce wedding festivities at the slightest opportunity. The term 'two armies' is the very same word used in *Genesis 32.2* where Jacob gave a place the name 'Mahanaim' (meaning two hosts or camps). The patriarch was returning home in obedience to God. Going in faith with his small army of family and servants he was apprehensive about the future, particularly about his reception by Esau, and God gave him a glimpse of an army of angels to powerfully comfort and assure him.

In the *Song*, the groom asks, 'What will the returning Shulamite be like? Mahanaim!' Two armies. The church will be one army, but the other will be the host of God. We are especially loved, defended, and strengthened when we return to His service. In a church we have no need of worldly entertainment to attract the lost. We do not have to compromise our standards and succumb to carnal wisdom in our methods. 'Come back to Me,' says the Lord, 'And take the power of My Spirit in the Word, for you are not alone, and a second and infinitely greater army is with you in the struggle for souls.'

The Mutual Love of Christ and His People

CHAPTER
7

A Believer's Personal Characteristics

1 'How beautiful are thy feet with shoes, O prince's daughter! the joints of thy thighs are like jewels, the work of the hands of a cunning workman.'

THE VIRTUES of the bride-to-be are now extolled even further by the groom, reminding us of the pleasure that Christ takes in His people, even though the characteristics He praises are those which He gave us Himself at conversion. He vested our souls with light and life, and loves us as His handiwork. Some interpreters liken each bodily feature here to a doctrine or to a promise of God, leading to heart-warming observations. But we feel that they refer more to features of the bride's conduct and character.

The groom's praises range from the feet to the head, beginning with the feet and shoes. It has been suggested that this 'lowliest' region of the body represents the believer's humility and modesty, so pleasant in the eyes of Christ. However, in the Bible shoes also represent mobility, the Lord having given His people power to move undaunted through all kinds of difficult terrain, with His help. We run to good works, and also to the place of prayer. We walk in the pilgrimage of faith and advance with our feet shod with the Gospel of peace to win the lost. Willing mobility, alacrity to obey Christ, is a great grace. Watts adapted *Psalm 119.57* to produce this hymn stanza –

> *Thou art my portion, O my God,*
> *I'm pledged to keep Thy way,*
> *To willingly obey Thy Word,*
> *And ACT without delay.*

Although a poor girl, her face burned by toil in the sun, the bride is called a 'prince's daughter', because her deportment and bearing are worthy of the royal family of the redeemed. She keeps herself pure and chaste for her groom just as we keep ourselves clear of the debased entertainment and television soaps of this world. Our minds will be kept for Christ. The bride has dignity, integrity, gracious speech, and a developed sense of responsibility. These things are instinctual for believers and must be prayed for and maintained. Do we watch our deportment that it may please the Lord?

The groom's reference to the joints of the bride's thighs does not suggest pre-marital intimacy, but the observation of her lithe, fluent movements. Some people are gifted with a natural athletic smoothness of action, while others run and move with noticeable jerkiness. The gifted ones seem to have well-oiled joints. The bride's effortless agility represents Christian grace, which is flexible and supple in response to trials, and in meeting the needs of others.

When we are assailed by problems and difficulties, do we panic and doubt, and become ill-tempered or self-pitying? Or do we respond with prayer and faith? Are we those who can uphold and help others in a crisis, or do we need to be supported ourselves? Sadly, churches are seen panicking today, lurching from gimmick to gimmick and from one worldly device to another to stem the decline in worshippers. Where is the grace, loved by Christ, of loyal faith in the power of the Word and the Spirit? Mobility in movement and gracious beauty are the twin themes of this verse.

2 'Thy navel is like a round goblet, which wanteth not liquor: thy belly is like an heap of wheat set about with lilies.'

THIS NAVEL verse is another example of a rather uncomplimentary remark (if the *Song* is intended as a literal love poem). If, however, the description is allegorical, picturing the nourishment and well-proportioned appearance of the church spiritually, it makes excellent sense. Here, then, is the part of the body which processes food, resembling a beautiful table goblet full of 'mixture' (the literal Hebrew), probably wine (weak wine being permitted to the people in those times). Pictured together with the wheat, the bride is seen to be well provided for, like the church with her spiritual food. Christ loves His people to be eager to learn, open to correction, and glad to be encouraged, valuing the impact of the Word upon their souls. He loves them when they love the doctrines of the Word, and particularly the many views of Himself.

Balanced spiritual eating is no doubt also in mind here. When this writer was young the tail-end of the prophecy fad was still in evidence, with speakers touring the churches armed with huge charts. Everyone was wild about it, and doctrine took a far lower place. Then, in many churches, the doctrines of grace came in, but often to the exclusion of evangelism and active service for the Lord. Later everyone seemed to be reading Francis Schaeffer and analysing the evolution of society. A serious problem arises when any teaching, however beneficial in itself, somehow commands the total attention of believers. To have an unbalanced diet is to be poorly fed, weak, and susceptible to sicknesses. The Lord loves to behold His people wanting 'all the counsel of God' both for their understanding and their active service.

3 'Thy two breasts are like two young roes that are twins.'

THE SYMBOLS of love and care render the church beautiful to Christ, especially when that love is unselfish, grateful, committed, and actively expressed in practical service. How Christ loves His people when they reflect on Him, adore Him, obey Him, and work for His cause on earth. He has made some to be exceptionally tough and resilient in body and personality, so that they may bear special burdens and endure. But He does not take great pleasure in them if they lose the tender core of a born-again person. Love, sympathy, gentleness, warmth and approachability must always be conspicuous in genuine Christian character.

4 'Thy neck is as a tower of ivory; thine eyes like the fishpools in Heshbon, by the gate of Bathrabbim: thy nose is as the tower of Lebanon which looketh toward Damascus.'

THE FUNCTION of the neck, as we have observed previously, is to hold high the head, signifying a dignified, resolute, principled life, resisting temptation and maintaining a good witness. It is a picture of firm faith and strong loyalty. Ivory speaks of strength, whereas whiteness its suggests that this strength does not eclipse that gentleness, courtesy and approachability we have just spoken of. Do we combine these virtues?

Eyes like fishpools are more difficult to understand. The reference may be to large and well-known ornamental pools by the entrance of a certain city, giving a visually refreshing welcome to hot and dusty travellers. Eyes are the 'point of meeting' between two people, the point of visual contact and recognition. By the meeting of eyes we acknowledge one another, and if we avert our eyes we may appear to snub or offend the other person. The eyes, then, welcome and engage a person, taking account of his needs. So the eyes of the church are attractive to needy and lost souls. Believers' eyes do not say, 'I am downhearted and tired of life,' but, 'I have life and peace, and I have warmth, sympathy, help and a saving message for those I encounter.' Christ loves to see this.

The nose is often a distinctive and distinguishing feature, and Christ loves a distinctiveness in His people which marks them out from the unbelieving world. Believers do not flex and mould themselves to fit decadent behaviour or surroundings, either at business or college. They do not run with the pack or majority, but they maintain wholesome, godly character wherever they are. Many so-called churches today have tragically abandoned the old distinction between things which are sacred and things which are profane, importing their worship culture from the entertainment world. Christ has made His people to be different, and He loves their distinctive characteristics. 'They are not of the world,' said the Lord, 'even as I am not of the world.' And in the letter of *James* we read: 'Whosoever therefore will be a friend of the world is the enemy of God.' To love Christ is to stand for the things He loves, and to avoid the things He detests.

5 'Thine head upon thee is like Carmel, and the hair of thine head like purple; the king is held in the galleries.'

THE BRIDE'S head is her glorious crown, like Mount Carmel renowned for its beauty. She is adorned with hair of remarkable colour. We have met this kind of description already, the head signifying the thoughtful and wise conduct of churches and believers. Do we react to ideas and events emotionally, or do we react in accordance with biblical principles? Do we carefully weigh in the light of Scripture the various ideas and proposals put before us, especially as churches, or do we stumble through life in a clumsy, unthinking way taking up every suggestion and fad? The Lord gave us a special infusion of spiritual maturity at conversion and He loves to see this still exercised in our decisions. The king being 'held in the galleries' is better rendered, 'the king is captivated by your tresses,' meaning that Christ is captivated by our orderly, trusting thoughts, and particularly in our praying. That is the idea of the passage if we are right in thinking that the hair, as an ornament of the head, pictures the noble function of the head as the seat of rationality and intelligence. In *2 Timothy 1.7* Paul says, 'For God hath not given us the spirit of fear; but of power, and of love, and of a sound mind.' The 'sound mind' is (in the Greek) the *safe* mind, well illustrated by the 'safe pair of hands' of the goalkeeper or wicket-keeper. Christ loves our safe-mindedness in times of stress or decision, by which we look to Him.

6 'How fair and how pleasant art thou, O love, for delights!'

WHEN THE GROOM sees his bride's beauties, his heart is moved, and when the Lord sees His people's graces exercised, and their spiritual character shining forth, His love is exercised very strongly towards them.

7 'This thy stature is like to a palm tree, and thy breasts to clusters of grapes.'

THERE ARE NO grapes in this verse (this word is in italics in the KJV) for the bride resembles a date palm, always upright and firm under pressure, always fruitful and evergreen. In the church these qualities are present by grace, and Christ loves the strengths He gives to be manifested. We cannot help thinking of the three 'stands' in *Ephesians 6.11-14*:

> 'Put on the whole armour of God, that ye may be able to stand against the wiles of the devil ... Wherefore take unto you the whole armour of God, that ye may be able to withstand in the evil day, and having done all, to stand. Stand therefore ...'

The palm tree picture is about standing for the Truth, standing against personal temptation, and standing courageously in witness to Christ.

8 'I said, I will go up to the palm tree, I will take hold of the boughs thereof: now also thy breasts shall be as clusters of the vine, and the smell of thy nose like apples.'

IN THIS LANGUAGE, the groom speaks of embracing his future bride and enjoying her love, no doubt in a chaste manner. The church cannot yet see the Saviour and hear His voice in a literal way, but He draws near to her, tells her how very close she may come by faith, and takes her in His arms. There is no greater assurance to a believer than to realise and remember that He is near, and that He welcomes and loves our love and utmost confidence in Him.

'But I do not *feel* assured,' someone may say. Then reflect deeply on this – that Christ loves His people, and particularly when they draw close, and trust themselves to Him. Assurance is primarily an attitude of faith, and our feeling of assurance is our glad response to this.

9 'And the roof of thy mouth like the best wine for my beloved, that goeth down sweetly, causing the lips of those that are asleep to speak.'

THE GROOM continues to speak of the sweetness of the bride's breath, then she interrupts (after the word 'wine'), saying (in effect), 'It is for you, my beloved, going sweetly (literally directly or smoothly) and gently to sleeping lips.' All her affections are for her groom, and when he praises her attributes she gives them all the more to him. This is a picture of the total consecration of the church to Christ. If He gives us gifts and graces, they are for Him. If He commends us for love, obedience and service, we will all the more devote these things to Him.

We learn from the bride a vitally helpful attitude that will strengthen us in all we do for Christ. To worship with my whole heart involves the work of summoning my thoughts and desires and fixing them on God alone. From where should I get motivation? Take, for example, the work of witnessing for Christ. This involves the suppressing of shyness or fear. From where will I get the incentive I need? Or take as another example the work of sanctification. This requires sacrifice and sometimes firm and painful self-denial. From where shall I obtain the necessary determination? The bride reveals her method for pleasing her groom in all things in this verse, saying, 'It is for you; it is what will please you.' That thought and aim will inspire motivation, incentive and determination for the whole spiritual walk. It is all for Christ, Who has purchased me, and Who I will soon see in glory. May we all learn to say daily, 'It is for my beloved.'

10 'I am my beloved's, and his desire is toward me.'

HERE THE BRIDE reveals an even more basic reason for her devotedness to the groom: it is the realisation that she belongs to him, and that he *wants* her. In relation to Christ, this is an unfathomably deep realisation, for why, why should He desire us, and make us His own to protect, mould and bless us? We cannot really understand the grace of God but we know it has embraced us, and the sense of privilege and amazement should never be allowed to slip away. We must think – He wants to bring me home, and watches me every step of my journey. He will inspire and strengthen my obedience and service as nothing else can. He died to save me, and will secure me eternally, and I will therefore abandon all my self-seeking and love of worldly satisfaction, and give myself unreservedly to Him.

11 'Come, my beloved, let us go forth into the field; let us lodge in the villages.'

UP TO THIS POINT the groom has always used the word 'Come!' but now the bride employs it, calling him to visit the countryside where his vineyards are. Evidently she has already been there (verse 13) and prepared some pleasures for him. They will lodge in the villages, clearly in separate places, because they are not yet married. We can almost hear the church prayer meeting calling upon the Lord: 'Come, Lord, into our harvest fields and vineyards to gather the fruit of precious souls.'

12 'Let us get up early to the vineyards; let us see if the vine flourish, whether the tender grape appear, and the pomegranates bud forth: there will I give thee my loves.'

THE BRIDE wants the groom's fruit to appear, and when they are surrounded by his interests and handiwork she will give him her love. In our churches we should not be saying, 'Raise and extend the platform, erect a gantry of spotlights, assemble an orchestra or a contemporary music band, bring in beautiful soloists and let us have fine entertainment and a good time.' We should be saying with the bride of the *Song*, 'Come, Lord, to a reverent place, where we may sing profound words, pray, and hear the Truth. Come to the place where fruit is seen in lives, and where we may have communion with Thee, and there we will give Thee all our love.'

Like the bride, true believers want to share the Lord's interests, non-essential earthly matters being of small importance. They want to be where they can exercise their powers in the cause of the Gospel, hearing it preached, praying for souls, and supporting the Sunday School outreach to the rising generation. They want to hear about the triumphs and trials of missionaries, and of the church in places of suffering. Christ's interests are theirs. They must be where souls are born anew, and lives built up – the vineyards of the Lord.

13 'The mandrakes give a smell, and at our gates are all manner of pleasant fruits, new and old, which I have laid up for thee, O my beloved.'

THE MANDRAKES (either love apples or the citron trees) signal readiness, picturing new graces and fresh advances ready to be surveyed by our divine Groom. It appears the bride-to-be has visited and gently moved around the farms and vineyards greeting the workers, and choosing the best of the early fruits to lay at the gates for when the groom comes. We see, yet again, that the best motive for achieving any advance in the Christian life is to do it to please the Lord. It is also the best sustaining force, giving patience and persistence to Christian workers. When in trouble and distress, the longing to please Christ is a most powerful help and incentive to process matters spiritually. The bride lays up pleasant fruits both old and new, and we will praise the Lord for past as well as present blessings, and also for the certainty of future blessings. We see how her love for the groom is expressed in practical deeds, preparing good things for him, and our love to Christ is also authenticated by fruits of holiness and Gospel service.

The Mutual Love of Christ and His People

A Believer's Prayers

1 'O that thou wert as my brother, that sucked the breasts of my mother! when I should find thee without, I would kiss thee; yea, I should not be despised.'

WE REMIND ourselves once again that the bride and groom had been bound to each other by an initial betrothal ceremony in accordance with the times, but they did not yet live together because their full wedding ceremony lay in the future. They lived in different places, and visited each other as often as possible, but they did not lie down together. This accurately represents the present age of the church before the second coming of Christ. He has come to redeem us and we are His people, 'married' to Him in a sense, but awaiting His glorious return and the great bridal supper of the Lamb, when all the church shall be gathered in, when faith shall be turned into sight, and unbroken communion will be our everlasting bliss.

The *Song* paints the picture of our present situation in which we know and relate to Christ by faith. Longing for the marriage day, the bride muses to herself in this verse, wishing that her groom was like a brother, because then, if she saw him arriving at her house to visit, she would rush out, throw her arms round him, and kiss him uninhibitedly, showing her love. But they are not married, and it would not be proper or seemly in their culture to engage in that form of outward love and affection.

Naturally believers desire closer fellowship with Christ even now, but not of an artificially worked-up, emotional kind. In his hymns, Charles Wesley frequently distinguishes between present and future communion, such as in the following verse:

> *Then, Saviour, then my soul receive,*
> *Transported from this earth to live*
> *And reign with Thee above;*
> *Where faith is sweetly lost in sight,*
> *And hope in full supreme delight,*
> *And everlasting love.*

Some Christians miss the point here. They seek after a sensational experience as though they could feel in some way that they had actually touched Christ, or felt His presence. They want an ecstatic, elevated, very tangible feeling, as if they were projected into the heavenlies even now. Some who try to achieve such a rapturous experience complain that to know Christ by faith is too cerebral, and not enough. They do not seem to know that communion by faith is very wonderful without trance-like, mystical sensations. It operates like this: we know Christ through the Word of God and the evidence of His power in our lives. We *reflect on* all that He has done, and on His wonderful character and love. As we value these things, then God, by His Spirit, touches our hearts to make these truths so real to us that our spirits are greatly warmed and our appreciation immensely deepened. There is no 'felt touch', but there is for us a remarkable realisation of Christ's love to us. The biblical rule is that all spiritual blessing is channelled to us through our conscious minds, and then our spirits rise, by the blessing of the Holy Spirit, in intelligent and feelingful appreciation of spiritual things.

Some time ago, speaking to a believer who fell to the ground under the experience of being 'slain in the Spirit', the writer asked what he was thinking about when it happened. 'Nothing,' was the reply, 'it was just a wonderful sensation.' He insisted that it had made him a better person, but he was unable to name any particular virtue he had received, or any sin conquered by it. His was simply an emotional and mystical experience produced by a 'technique', and this is not what we are given in the Christian faith. The rule of the New Testament is that all our spiritual joy and experience is 'by faith'. We wait for the 'wedding' for faith to become sight.

2 'I would lead thee, and bring thee into my mother's house, who would instruct me: I would cause thee to drink of spiced wine of the juice of my pomegranate.'

STILL MUSING to herself the bride visualises how she would lead her groom to her home to show him her own 'domain'. This presents an unusual factor, for we think of being led *by* Christ, yet here the bride wants to lead the groom. Theologically it is not the right way round, but it is what often happens in courtship. The lady wants to take the man to her place and to her surroundings and show him her world. And in a sense we lead Christ into our affairs. It is a great privilege for us to do so, and it is very condescending of Him to allow us to do so. We lead Him into our prayer agenda, our concerns, our devotions and our lives. How gracious is the everlasting Son of God to come into our affairs! If we do not lead Him there He may not come and we will miss the blessings of communion and answered prayer.

'Who would instruct me' (referring to the bride's mother) is better rendered – 'who instructed me' – indicating that chaste behaviour was her training. In her home she would give him wine flavoured with her own fruits. Wine was permitted to the people of God in those days. It was a very weak product, used sparingly, and even diluted. But the point here is that she wants to please him and make something special for him. These are exactly the sentiments of the church of Christ, and of believers in particular – or should be.

We should want to live for His pleasure, and strive to make our thoughts acceptable to the One Who watches us constantly and is aware of all that is in our minds. At times when our thoughts are free to rove what do we think about? Are our thoughts angry and against others? Are we absorbed in earthly desires, or self-concern? Let us lead Christ into our 'world' or life, and do and think to bring pleasure to Him.

3 'His left hand should be under my head, and his right hand should embrace me.'

IF WE ARE trying to please Christ, then the experience of this verse will follow, and we will know more of His kindness directing our lives. The hand under the head is, of course, allegorical, meaning that He will guide us in our thoughts and plans, and bless our understanding. His embrace is a picture of assurance and comfort. If we desire this direction and assurance then we must first 'lead Him' into the place of prayer and communion, and try to please Him.

4 'I charge you, O daughters of Jerusalem, that ye stir not up, nor awake my love, until he please.'

THESE WORDS are spoken to the bride's maidens-in-waiting by either the bride or the groom; the Hebrew strictly favours the latter, and this is in line with the two previous occurrences of this same sentiment. The maidens are directed not to wake the bride, which means they must not disturb her while she is engaged in reflection, love and devotion. This must never be displaced, even by such crucial activities as evangelism or teaching. The idea is this: there are times for service, for witness, for daily work, and for study, but times of devotion and communion must always keep their honoured place and be free from unnecessary interruptions. Do not omit them, and do not spoil them by bad moods. Curb and correct anything that would cause the skipping or slipping of devotions.

> 5 'Who is this that cometh up from the wilderness, leaning upon her beloved? I raised thee up under the apple tree: there thy mother brought thee forth: there she brought thee forth that bare thee.'

A DRAMATIC change of theme arrives with this verse, all spoken, we think, by the bride, who in the first sentence takes up the words spoken by her maidens in chapter 3 verse 6. Previously she was in the groom's chariot or sedan, coming out of the wilderness towards the city where the wedding would take place (although the narrative stops short of the great event).

The bride now reminds herself that her life is 'travelling' to a wedding. No chariot is mentioned because her dependence upon her groom is the key matter here. She sees herself as having left the outlying wild country and entered the farmlands and orchards around the city. As before, she represents the church gathered out of the world, now with Christ on the way to the wedding.

> 'Jesus suffers no pilgrim on the road to the New Jerusalem to travel unattended. He is with us. When we least perceive Him, He is often closest to us. When the howling tempest drowns His voice, still He is there.'
>
> – C. H. Spurgeon

The Hebrew for 'leaning' means depending. Only the groom could bring her from the wilderness to the town. She had been held in virtual captivity by her brothers and made to work in their vineyards, neglecting her own little patch, until scorched by the sun.

She had no livelihood or property or place in the city; no means of getting there and then surviving, and so she was entirely dependent upon her groom to bring her from her distant home. Is this not a perfect picture of the elect possessing no righteousness by which to deserve Heaven, and entangled in this evil world? But Christ sets His love upon us, saves us, and brings us to Himself so that we lean upon Him and His work for us. The words of Isaac Watts follow this traditional interpretation of the verse:

> Who is this loved one in distress
> Who travels from the wilderness,
> And pressed with sorrows and with sins,
> On her belovèd Lord she leans?
>
> This is the bride of Christ our God,
> Bought with the treasures of His blood;
> And all her supplications there
> Picture each saint in tender prayer.

The second part of verse 5 is notably mysterious, but from among the old favourites we suggest the following explanation. The apple tree probably represents the place of love, the orchard, with its special aroma, and so the idea is that the bride's mind goes back to the time when she first loved the groom. 'I raised thee up,' she says, meaning that she awakened his love, and this is a precious memory for her. So it is for us in connection with Christ. It is true we love Him because He first loved us, but from our subjective point of view, it seems as though we approached Him, and from that time He 'awoke' and blessed us. In reality, we were spiritually dead, ignorant, and totally disinclined to come to Christ, but by His invisible drawing we did so, and found His forgiving love.

The groom's mother bringing him forth is probably also a figure for love, because a child is ideally born through love. The groom came into her life as suddenly as a babe, through the operation of love.

6 'Set me as a seal upon thine heart, as a seal upon thine arm: for love is strong as death; jealousy is cruel as the grave: the coals thereof are coals of fire, which hath a most vehement flame.'

WHETHER bride and groom have now met up, or whether this is her reflecting, or whether she has sent him a message, we cannot tell, but these very beautiful words are the desire of her heart. 'Take me as a precious possession,' she pleads, or perhaps the seal is a medallion or ring, or something with her name upon it to be worn on his person to constantly remind him of her. And this is just what the church and the individual believer prays to Christ, 'Set me in Thy love Lord, and do not put me away because of my sin and foolishness. Bless me and be kind to me always.' But, of course, we know He will be. He will never turn His heart or His mind away from His people. The seal is here a pledge of permanence, and we rejoice in the doctrine of eternal perseverance. The lines of Watts express once again the prayer of the bride:

> O let my name engraven stand,
> My Jesus, on Thy heart and hand:
> Seal me upon Thine arm, and wear
> That pledge of love for ever there.

God's arm normally speaks of His work, and particularly His protective power, reminding us of the grand words of Philip Doddridge:

> Zion, Jehovah's portion and delight,
> Graven on His hands, and hourly in His sight.

Halfway through verse 6 the bride describes their love, but his love is primarily in her mind. In what way is love as 'strong as death'? Death is so powerful it claims everyone, none being immune whether rich or poor, powerful or of no consequence. Death is irresistible and the love of Christ is the same. If His love is upon us we will be loved with all His gracious intensity through life and eternity, because nothing can overpower His love or turn it aside.

The next sentiment explains the strength of Christ's love. He is jealous for His people, meaning that He will not share us with the world or the devil or hell, and if necessary He will chastise us if we go chasing worldly, sinful things. The grave is hard in that it is unyielding. You cannot plead with it to give a person back, not even for a few days. The *King James* translators chose the word 'cruel' for poetic power, but the Hebrew means *hard* or unyielding, and so is the 'jealousy' of God for the loyalty and safety of His people.

'Coals of fire' points to love which is unquenchable for ever, and full of passion and expression. The love of Christ toward us is constantly expressed by Him in privileges, kindnesses and gracious interventions in our lives. The end of verse 6 is translated by some modern translations in this way: 'like the very flame of the Lord', and the Hebrew does use a form of the divine name. Our *King James* translators have backed away from this, possibly in reverence, as the name of God is used nowhere else in the *Song*. However, this writer feels that the name of the Lord is intended, and that the 'flame kindled by the Lord' is the eternal, unquenchable love of Christ for His people.

7 'Many waters cannot quench love, neither can the floods drown it: if a man would give all the substance of his house for love, it would utterly be contemned.'

SADLY, in the case of human love, it may be quenched by betrayal and drowned by sorrows. Even at its best it is not always stable, although we recognise that courtship and married love can and should be very powerful and deep. But the *Song* ultimately speaks of Christ's love which cannot be extinguished by all the oceans and rivers in the world. When sin entered into the world it drowned love for God, and self-love gained a foothold in human lives rendering us incapable of acceptable love for God, and frequently for other people also. Love for this present world became rampant, and worst of all the love of sin. 'How sad our state by nature is!'

But the love of Christ is so strong, pure and gracious that His people are never forgotten, and nothing will ever cause that love to diminish. If only our love could rise to His, even to some extent! We must desire greater love for Him, and respond to His love much more than we do, watching out for those earthly factors that blunten it or steal it away. How majestically Watts captures the sense of the bride's words:

> Stronger than death Thy love is known,
> Which many floods could never drown;
> And hell and earth in vain combine
> To quench a fire so much divine.

Verse 7 goes on to say that if one tried to buy love, even with all one's wealth, it would be scorned. We might lavish gifts on a person to draw their love from someone else, but the object of our attention will despise our strategy. In relation to Christ, we cannot buy His love by saying, 'Lord, love me, for I've done good works.' His love must be given to us freely. But does not Christ lavish the riches of salvation on us to 'buy' our love? Of course not, for the gift of salvation does not buy our *love*, it purchases *us*, and then He pours love into our hearts. He did not bribe us to love Him, but changed our hearts to make us those who love Him. But that gift of love must be exercised by us or it will grow cold.

8 'We have a little sister, and she hath no breasts: what shall we do for our sister in the day when she shall be spoken for?'

SOME MODERN Bible versions tell us that it is the bride's brothers speaking, and others say it is the maidens, but we believe it is the bride either describing the attitude of her brothers toward her when she was younger, or (another interpretation) asking the groom what will become of her own little sister after the marriage.

The first interpretation, which we think is best, is that the bride is recounting the unscrupulous way in which her brothers had aimed to exploit her. We have seen how they made her work for them, but they also said to each other, 'What shall we do for this little girl when she grows up?'

9 'If she be a wall, we will build upon her a palace of silver: and if she be a door, we will inclose her with boards of cedar.'

'THIS IS WHAT we will do,' they said. 'If she is a wall, we will build upon her a palace of silver,' meaning, if she is easily controlled and we can keep a wall around her, then we will put a huge dowry price on her head. This would achieve one of two outcomes. Either, no one would be able to afford her, in which case she would remain their servant or slave for life, or, if someone could afford her, the brothers would make a lot of money. If, however, she grew up to be a 'door', uncontrollable and out and about with a mind of her own, the brothers would force her to stay with them by strategies to fence her in, so that their aim would not be thwarted.

10 'I am a wall, and my breasts like towers: then was I in his eyes as one that found favour.'

'THIS WAS MY situation,' says the bride, 'for I was virtually locked in a fortress. But then I found favour in the eyes of one more powerful than my brothers, who brought me out.' If this is what the bride is saying, it certainly parallels the experience of Christ's people. We were in the world, and the world held us, walling us in, but Christ paid the price, and He took us for Himself.

But here is another interpretation. Back in verse 8, the bride is saying that she really does have in her family a little sister who faces an uncertain future. 'What will become of her?' she asks. According to this interpretation, the groom then replies (verse 9) saying, 'Don't worry, we will take care of her future together, and we will turn her into a palace and protect her.' The application of this would be along these lines: the convert to Christ brings before the Lord in prayer the situation of brothers and sisters or any others dear to them, and asks what will become of them, and the Lord says, 'We are together, and if you lay them before Me, I will take account of them.' This application would not guarantee their conversion, but it would amount to an invitation to intercede for them. It is the promise of a special hearing. Whichever of these interpretations is correct, both applications are true. There are, of course, other interpretations, but in our view none are as likely or as edifying.

11 'Solomon had a vineyard at Baal-hamon; he let out the vineyard unto keepers; every one for the fruit thereof was to bring a thousand pieces of silver.'

THE LOCATION of Baal-hamon is immaterial, but the name means master or possessor of many. The name may hint at the vastness of the groom's possessions, as extensive as Solomon's – hence the choice of the king's name as a symbol of the groom. More significant is the arrangement that vineyard keepers must each pay a rent of a thousand pieces of silver.

12 'My vineyard, which is mine, is before me: thou, O Solomon, must have a thousand, and those that keep the fruit thereof two hundred.'

NOW THE BRIDE was a poor woman whose own neglected vineyard was small and produced little. We assume that the vineyard which she speaks about had been given to her by the groom, perhaps as a betrothal present, or as a gift of love. She is looking at it as she speaks these words, either literally or in her mind, and she wants to give the groom the same rent as his tenants, meaning that she will obey him and serve him as they do, but willingly and gladly. She will deduct only the fair wages of her own vineyard tenders, and everything she produces will be for him. So the new believer, and hopefully the veteran believer also, says to the

Lord, 'Everything that I have received is for Thee, and I hereby dedicate it to Thee.' This is the language of real conversion and love for Christ:

> *My life I bring to Thee,*
> *I would not be my own;*
> *O Saviour, may I be*
> *Thine ever, Thine alone!*
> *My heart, my life, my all, I bring*
> *To Thee, my Saviour and my King.*

13 'Thou that dwellest in the gardens, the companions hearken to thy voice: cause me to hear it.'

SURELY this is the groom speaking, telling the bride that their times of companionship in the beautiful garden of communion are in his mind and on his heart. He reminds her that she speaks often and shares much with the daughters of Jerusalem, the maidens-in-waiting. Through the *Song* they have heard her words, and this is right. In the church we speak often to one another, and we explain the things of Christ to others, giving particular help to seekers and young believers. We discuss our blessings and woes with our close friends, but in this *Song* the groom says gently to the bride (exactly as the Lord says to us), 'Speak to me also. Talk to me, as you talk to them. Talk to me, not just mechanically or nominally, uttering the same few things every day, but tell me and ask me everything.' Love speaks to the one loved, and by much prayer we both express and exercise love to Christ. We could collect from the bride's conversations in the *Song* a

> 'The *Song* is almost ended: the bride and groom are about to part for a while. They utter their adieux, and the groom says to his beloved ... "When I am far away, fill this garden with my name, and let my heart commune with thee." She promptly replies, and it is her last word till he comes, "Make haste, my beloved ..."'
>
> – C. H. Spurgeon

range of joys and trials, and to them all Christ says – 'Bring them to Me.' All should be spread before the Lord, the implicit promise being that He will respond.

14 'Make haste, my beloved, and be thou like to a roe or to a young hart upon the mountains of spices.'

WITHOUT DOUBT this last verse is the bride's. We have seen these remarkable terms before, and we know what they mean. 'Make haste, Lord,' she says, 'and come like an energetic roe or young hart (literally a gazelle and a young stag) leaping upon those dangerous, dividing mountains, yet with sure footing.' Far away and inaccessible, these hills are nevertheless beautiful, for they represent the next life and the glories of Heaven. The meaning is that every believer should be growing and deepening in desire for Christ and for Heaven. We must look forward to the day when we will be with Him, or to the day when He will come in power and glory. If we look forward to the eternal glory this world will shrink in our estimation, but if we forget Heaven for any length of time, this world will grow in our estimation and we will dream of its pleasures and rewards. Let us keep the flame of love for Heaven alive in our thoughts.

Literally the bride says, 'Flee away, my beloved,' but we must read it as, 'Come away quickly.' 'Even so,' we read at the very end of the Bible, 'Come, Lord Jesus.' Soon, we shall see the end of all rebellion and suffering. Soon we shall witness the dramatic end of this age of intense opposition to high and holy things, and see the great day of vindication for Christ, our Saviour.

This is what we should look forward to above all else, for this is the ultimate purpose of all our labour and soul-winning – to gather people for that great day. Have we become fixed on this world? Do our roots go down too far into its doomed soil? Do we shudder a little at the idea that this present life will soon end? What a profound shame! May we pray more for a strong desire for the future, and be moved to work in the vineyard of our divine Groom, bringing in the harvest of souls for the greatest and ultimate day of earth's history. That will be the day of the long-awaited wedding: the marriage supper of the Lamb.

The Mutual Love of Christ and His People

Epilogue
The Believer's Hope

EVERY ASPECT of the amazing love of Christ for His people is to be found reflected in this *Song of Songs*. It tells of how He set His love upon us, came and found us, paid dearly for us, stirred our willing love, brought us away from the place of exploitation and oppression, dealt graciously with us, and filled our minds with the prospect of a glorious eternity. Every aspect of the love of the true church is also found in the *Song*. It tells of our discovery of Christ, our consciousness of utter unworthiness, our commitment and vows to Him, our forsaking of this world, our communion, devotion and service, our growth in grace through times of failure and re-establishment, and our longing to cross the mountains of division to see Him and be with Him for ever.

We hear in this *Song* of His unfathomable love for us, and we are overwhelmed by His grace and lovingkindness. To reflectively study the *Song* brings us back to our first and foremost love, so that we say with Watts (in lines inspired by chapter 8) –

> *Till Thou hast brought me to Thy home*
> *Where fears and doubts can never come,*
> *Let me Thy count'nance often see*
> *As daily I draw near to Thee.*

There is one more hymn of Watts from which we must quote verses as we close this devotional study, because this also was inspired by the *Song of Solomon*. Here is the believer's hope, and the communion of enlightened love:

> *How soon! my God, my joys shall rise*
> *   And run eternal rounds,*
> *Beyond the limits of the skies,*
> *   And all created bounds.*
>
> *There, where my Saviour, Jesus, reigns,*
> *   In Heaven's unmeasured space,*
> *I'll spend a long eternity*
> *   In pleasure and in praise.*
>
> *Millions of years my wondering eyes,*
> *   Shall o'er Thy beauties rove;*
> *And endless ages I'll adore,*
> *   The glories of Thy love.*
>
> *Dear Jesus, every smile of Thine*
> *   Shall fresh endearments bring;*
> *And thousand tastes of new delight*
> *   From all Thy graces spring.*
>
> *Haste, my Belov'd, and take my soul*
> *   Up to Thy blest abode:*
> *Come, for my spirit longs to see*
> *   My Saviour and my God.*

Appendix
How Psalm 45 Parallels the Song as Allegorical

Psalm 45 has often been called the key to the *Song of Solomon* as it employs a very similar style of description, featuring the marriage of a great king and the splendour of his court. Traditionally regarded as a Messianic psalm, the first half leaves one in no doubt that the king referred to is a divine person. This is confirmed by *Hebrews 1.8-9*, where Christ's divinity is proved by reference to this psalm.

If the first half of the psalm is unmistakably about the Messiah, then the second half (describing the wedding) must be an allegorical description of the bond between Christ and His bride – the church. No other interpretation is credible. And if *Psalm 45* is allegorical, then so is the *Song of Solomon* which runs along the same lines, although the wedding is left to the future.

Verses 1-7 describe Messiah

We begin by establishing that *Psalm 45* describes the Messiah, the Son of God. Some commentaries strenuously attempt to stretch the words of the psalm to fit an earthly king, but the descriptions are far too lofty. For example, where verse 2 says that this king will be blessed for ever, the more

114 The Mutual Love of Christ and His People

liberal kind of commentaries claim this refers to his dynasty; his sons. However, such an interpretation treats the Bible as a fallible – even naive – book, because the unbroken and continual godliness and blessing of a king's sons has never happened, and could never happen because of human sinfulness.

Verse 2: The king is described as being outstanding among men, exceptional in benevolence, and blessed by God for all time – words which would never 'fit' an earthly king, including Solomon who painfully overtaxed the people, and fell from godliness and success for much of his life. 'A greater than Solomon is here.'

Verse 3: This king (unlike Solomon) is a mighty warrior of great glory, more like David, but far too great to be him.

Verse 4: This warrior king is always victorious, and fights to vindicate truth, humility and righteousness – the work of Christ in fulfilling prophecies, humbling Himself on Calvary to save others, and offering up His righteousness to earn and secure their blessing. In accordance with this verse, when Christ came He demonstrated His divinity by the most awesome miracles.

Verse 5: This king evidently uses not real arrows, but arrows of conviction, because the previous verse calls his warfare an expedition of *meekness*. By Christ's appeal of kindness, people of all nations fall beneath His feet. No purely human warrior ever worked like this, only the God-man, Jesus Christ our Lord.

Verse 6: Lest we should be in the slightest doubt that the One spoken of is God, the psalmist now says so plainly. (This and the next are the verses quoted in *Hebrews 1.8-9.*)

Verse 7: Father and Son are both clearly in this verse (see again *Hebrews 1.8-9*). 'Fellows' may refer to all the noble and royal guests at the wedding depicted in the psalm, perhaps representing all the prophets, apostles and preachers of the church, for Christ is far above them all.

Verses 8-17 describe the attributes and blessings of both king and bride

Verse 8: If the great king of the psalm is Christ, which is surely indisputable, then the language now becomes a figurative description of His attributes and perfections – drawn from wedding garments and palace furnishings.

Verse 9: Many of the guests come from Gentile lands, picturing the calling of the Gentiles to Christ. The bride is first mentioned here.

Verse 10: The bride is addressed and exhorted, and if the king is Christ then the bride is His church – people called to leave their old country (or life) and follow Christ as their King.

Verse 11: The called out people are beautiful in Christ's sight (through converting grace) and they are to bow themselves down before Him (the *KJV* use of 'worship' is fully justified; the *NIV* 'honour him' is weak).

Verse 12: The kingdom of Tyre first recognised David, and represents here all people who bow to the reign of Christ and seek His face.

Verse 13: The bride, pictured as a princess, is further described. She is viewed in the very throne room of the inner palace as glorious, and richly clad in the righteousness of Christ.

Verse 14: So clad she will be brought to the king with her companions (surely the same as the maidens-in-waiting of the *Song of Solomon*).

Verse 15: The wedding will be a day of great rejoicing.

Verse 16: A new order will come, with the church spread throughout the earth – surely referring to the church age – when the 'children' of the bride (the church) will accomplish by the Spirit greater things than those in the Jewish age.

Verse 17: The name of this king will dominate all generations.

Throughout this psalm an earthly event, the marriage of a Jewish king to a foreign princess, is described, but no earthly king is named or referred to, nor was any grand or glorious enough to merit the language used. It is Christ and His church who are described, just as in the *Song of Solomon*. It is true that in this psalm there is a wedding, and not in the *Song*, but the allegorical style of the one authenticates the style of the other.

Physicians of Souls
The Gospel Ministry
285 pages, paperback, ISBN 1 870855 34 5

'Compelling, convicting, persuasive preaching, revealing God's mercy and redemption to dying souls, is seldom heard today. The noblest art ever granted to our fallen human race has almost disappeared.'

Even where the free offer of the Gospel is treasured in principle, regular evangelistic preaching has become a rarity, contends the author. These pages tackle the inhibitions, theological and practical, and provide powerful encouragement for physicians of souls to preach the Gospel. A vital anatomy or order of conversion is supplied with advice for counselling seekers.

The author shows how passages for evangelistic persuasion may be selected and prepared. He also challenges modern church growth techniques, showing the superiority of direct proclamation. These and other key topics make up a complete guide to soulwinning.

God's Rules for Holiness
139 pages, paperback, ISBN 1 870855 37 X

Taken at face value the Ten Commandments are binding on all people, and will guard the way to Heaven, so that evil will never spoil its glory and purity. But the Commandments are far greater than their surface meaning, as this book shows.

They challenge us as Christians on a still wider range of sinful deeds and attitudes. They provide positive virtues as goals. And they give immense help for staying close to the Lord in our walk and worship.

The Commandments are vital for godly living and for greater blessing, but we need to enter into the panoramic view they provide for the standards and goals for redeemed people.

Heritage of Evidence

127 pages, paperback, ISBN 1 870855 39 6

In today's atheistic climate most people have no idea how much powerful evidence exists for the literal accuracy and authenticity of the biblical record. The British Museum holds a huge number of major discoveries that provide direct corroboration and background confirmation for an immense sweep of Bible history. This survey of Bible-authenticating exhibits has been designed as a guide for visitors, and also to give pleasure and interest to readers unable to tour the galleries. It will also be most suitable for people who need to see the accuracy and inspiration of the Bible.

The 'tour' followed here started life over forty years ago and has been used by many thousands of people including youth and student groups.

Almost every item viewed on the tour receives a full colour photograph. Room plans are provided for every gallery visited showing the precise location of artefacts, and time-charts relate the items to contemporary kings and prophets. The book is enriched by pictures and descriptions of famous 'proofs' in other museums.

Worship in the Melting Pot

148 pages, paperback, ISBN 1 870855 33 7

'Worship is truly in the melting pot,' says the author. 'A new style of praise has swept into evangelical life shaking to the foundations traditional concepts and attitudes.' How should we react? Is it all just a matter of taste and age? Will churches be helped, or changed beyond recognition?

This book presents four essential principles which Jesus Christ laid down for worship, and by which every new idea must be judged.

Here also is a fascinating view of how they worshipped in Bible times, including their rules for the use of instruments, and the question is answered – What does the Bible teach about the content and order of a service of worship today?

The Lord's Pattern for Prayer

118 pages, paperback, ISBN 1 870855 36 1

Subtitled – 'Studying the lessons and spiritual encouragements in the most famous of all prayers.' This volume is almost a manual on prayer, providing a real spur to the devotional life. The Lord's own plan and agenda for prayer – carefully amplified – takes us into the presence of the Father, to prove the privileges and power of God's promises to those who pray.

Chapters cover each petition in the Lord's Prayer. Here, too, are sections on remedies for problems in prayer, how to intercede for others, the reasons why God keeps us waiting for answers, and the nature of the prayer of faith.

Also by Dr. Masters and in print from Wakeman:

Men of Purpose
197 pages, illustrated, paperback, ISBN 1 870855 41 8

Do We Have a Policy?
For Church Health and Growth
93 pages, paperback, ISBN 1 870855 30 2

The Healing Epidemic
227 pages, paperback, ISBN 1 870855 00 0

Only One Baptism of the Holy Spirit
109 pages, paperback, ISBN 1 870855 17 5

Steps for Guidance
184 pages, paperback, ISBN 1 870855 19 1

The Charismatic Phenomenon [co-authored with John C. Whitcomb]
113 pages, paperback, ISBN 1 870855 01 9

www.wakemantrust.org